REDHOTCHILIPEPPERS
SUGARANDSPICE

CHRISWATTS

Published by Castle Communications Plc
Book Division, A29 Barwell Business Park
Leatherhead Road, Chessington, Surrey KT9 2NY

Copyright © 1994 Castle Communications Plc

Book Design: Brian Burrows
Cover Design: Hugh Gilmour
Picture Research: Kay Rowley

ISBN 1 898141 03 7

RED**HOT**CHILI**PEPPERS**
SUGAR**AND**SPICE

TABLE**OF**CONTENTS

Chapter 1

It took 25 years for the stupid hippies to make it back to Max Yasgur's field. The old hippies made it back to take their old drugs, watch their old bands and celebrate a quarter of a century of nothing. The young hippies made it down to Woodstock II because the old hippies would never shut up about it all. The young hippies got to a field in up-State New York only to witness the main stage painted like the set of a particularly childish TV show.

Woodstock II was a cultural farce. The new age of Aquarius came to fruition courtesy of a cola corporation and a lightweight designer beer. Free love now cost 135 bucks and the money still couldn't stop the toilets from overflowing. It was estimated that the on-site stalls had to sell 60,000 pizzas each over the weekend just to cover the cost of renting the space from the festival organisers.

Two More Days Of Peace & Music? Maybe the event logo – two fat doves squatting smugly on a guitar neck – was a badly-drawn message to the assembled masses from the yuppy promoters. If an ex-lawyer and an ex-Wall Street achiever could mug a generation once, then their children would probably be stupid enough to get fooled again. No hard feelings, and the groovy rock'n'roll President himself was probably catching the vibes from the constant coverage on MTV. Bill Clinton, after all, had had hot sax with Stevie Nicks and invited Soul Asylum to play in his front garden since moving his liberal ticket into the White House.

The President, however, did not have to screw his wife in a mud bath or change his dollars up into 'Greedstock's own currency. With a wallet bulging with generally useless Scrip – money that could only be converted back into dollars at the end of the festival providing you could produce receipts for every pizza and love bead – you could buy an umbrella. It rained forever at Woodstock II. Festivals are still the great opiate for the gullible pop consumer. Sedated by the notion that festivals are something of a communion fired by tribal free spirit, the little baby innocents watch a procession of white rock pomp shouting dumb statements at them with a certain easy authority. Rock bands cannot change the '90s, just as they couldn't change the '80s or the '70s or even the fucking '60s, because they're too pussy to join an army and blow shit up.

But 325,000 people came down to the small town of Saugerties for Woodstock II anyway. Such supernova thickets as Metallica (overblown pomp speed metallers and born stadium bores), Aerosmith (40-something Himbos peddling Rod Stewart-approved sex anthems) and Green Day (cheque book new punks and as crap as The Damned), all performed under the giant rainbow on the main stage like so many corporate puppet-trolls.

REDHOTCHILIPEPPERS
SUGARANDSPICE

In 1969, The Who's Pete Townshend smashed his guitar over the head of a political anarchist who jumped up on stage for an impromptu anti-government rant. It was a gesture more in tune with the general air of malevolence generated at the Altamont festival just six months later. But in 1994 Pete Townshend was deaf and playing acoustic guitar in a bubble to protect his shattered hearing. The new breed are as comatose as their message ('Rock The Vote' and wishy-washy anti-porn lobbies). In this field they celebrated an atrocious nostalgia.

Woodstock II, then, was an incongruous setting in which to re-launch the Party Animal. The sky was darkening over Saugerties and the mud thickening. Nothing was being achieved and nothing was turning out to be expensive.

And then the Red Hot Chili Peppers took the main stage dressed as giant light bulbs.

Chapter 2

Punk rock surfaced in Los Angeles to destroy Fleetwood Mac. In 1979, British punk was crap. It was over. It could no longer shock. Instead the British punks had grown up and decided to write truckloads of cute pop songs for BBC Radio 1. Punk was now the new wave – Elvis Costello's 'Oliver's Army', Tom Robinson's 'Power In The Darkness', Eddie & The Hot Rods' 'Do Anything You Wanna Do', the Boomtown Rats' 'Rat Trap'... smalltown Everymen talking fondly about (horrors!) John Lennon and Bob Dylan, whilst sweeping into one-hit power on the coat-tails of the London pioneers. Punk rock was no longer threatening when you could whistle it on the way to the dole office.

But inspired by the antisocial arrogance of the Sex Pistols' cultural nihilism, the American underground still saluted punk rock. In Los Angeles it rose rapidly to sneer at the psychedelic boutiques along Melrose, and to curse the city's hippy residue. To the disaffected street youth living on the wrong side of the 'city of angels', punk was a vehicle for confrontation.

The Californian punks had no need for peace, love and understanding. Unlike the more literate scenesters from New York – the likes of Patti Smith, Television and Richard Hell – West Coast punk was a forearm smash of malevolence and dumb despair.

The punks formed co-ops to beat the one drum they all had in common. These co-ops had names that today sound quaint and cheesy: the Bags, the Weirdos, the Germs, the Alleycats, the Plugz... charmless names adopted for their utter mediocrity. And the LA establishment hated them.

The middle-aged cocaine fiends and celebrity soft rock power brokers began to blame punk for any civil misdemeanour. The police responded and grabbed every opportunity to beat punk back under the carpet. The cops swooped on the clubs – padlocking the doors of the notorious Masque dive and invading the Elks Lodge venue to club innocent by-standers with batons and night-sticks. The scale of conflict continued to escalate. The ferocity on both sides gave birth to a longer-lasting and infinitely more intimidating subculture.

Hardcore came to bury everything.

Ex-Big Chief vocalist, Barry Henssler, said hardcore came to "scrape off the Styxs and the Speedwagons and the remnant punk bullshit. Only when that was done could people get on with something different."

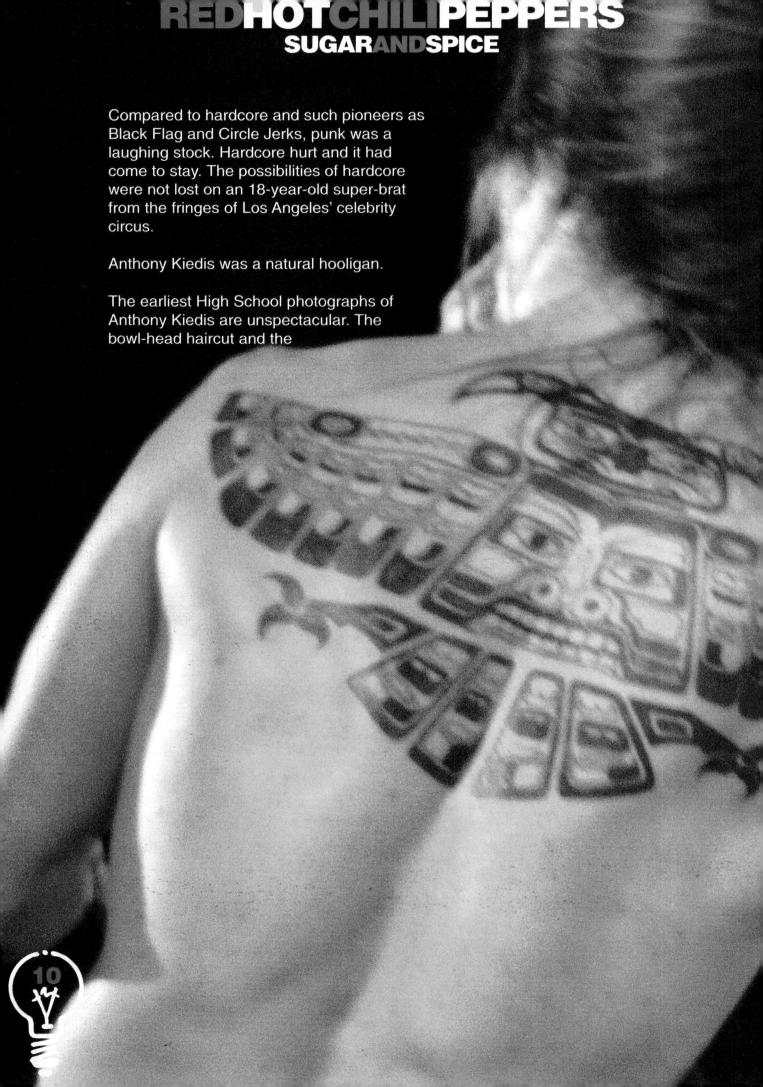

REDHOTCHILIPEPPERS
SUGARANDSPICE

Compared to hardcore and such pioneers as
Black Flag and Circle Jerks, punk was a
laughing stock. Hardcore hurt and it had
come to stay. The possibilities of hardcore
were not lost on an 18-year-old super-brat
from the fringes of Los Angeles' celebrity
circus.

Anthony Kiedis was a natural hooligan.

The earliest High School photographs of
Anthony Kiedis are unspectacular. The
bowl-head haircut and the

10

"Hardcore came to scrape off the Styxs and the Speedwagons and the remnant punk bullshit. Only when that was done could people get on with something different."

Sunday School collar and tie, all conspire to make Kiedis look like an angel page-boy. The image could not be further from the truth.

When asked a decade later what he'd wanted to be as a kid, he replied:

"An outlaw living on Sunset Strip, hanging out with the guys and doing what the hell I wanted to do."

At the age of 11, Anthony left his mother in Michigan and went to live with his father in Hollywood. His parents had separated amicably when he was a young child but his father had kept in touch, serenading his son with sunny tales of life in the fast lane as a partially successful movie scenester. Working under the name of Blackie Dammett, Kiedis senior never progressed beyond hammy B-movies but would always be able to pay the rent. In Los Angeles, paying the rent constitutes major success. To Anthony, his father's life was one long party. And Michigan was cold.

Anthony would later describe his father as: "your basic semi-subversive underground hooligan playboy womaniser type of character. He definitely had a strong influence on me."

So father and son were re-united in a city that seemed to offer a limitless buffet of hedonistic delights. Blackie Dammett arranged schooling for his son. He also arranged a one-way ticket to Hollywood Babylon.

At the age of 12, Anthony Kiedis lost his virginity to 18-year-old Kimberley Smith. She was also Blackie's girl for one night.

Later Anthony would describe the experience to Details magazine. "Never before had I felt my mind, body and spirit come together in an erotic effort that transcended all the bullshit and suffering of life."

The parties thrown by Blackie in the small flat father and son shared together were orgiastic and indulgent. But they were also hyper-fun.

"It seemed that every night in that apartment," Anthony remembers today, "was an endless stream of fights, drugs, and lots of guys and girls getting crazy. He (Blackie) had a constant turnover of girlfriends. He had this insatiable desire to meet all the beautiful girls in the world.

"It was the greatest thing in the world to have all these beautiful women come into my house and not be uptight about me hanging out with them."
The lifestyle was frivolous and fancy, but hardly stable. Today Kiedis admits that it was a privilege open to abuse.

"His steady turnover of women desensitised me towards wanting to attain true love with a single partner. With my not necessarily unwarranted sense of self-confidence, I was constantly attempting to unite with a woman."

To Anthony Kiedis, life was basically "anarchy on a plate".

In 1977, he was accepted by Fairfax High School and enrolled grudgingly. The tall but true tales of his fantasy lifestyle immediately marked him out as a novelty.

The first time Anthony Kiedis encountered Michael 'Flea' Balzary, the two kicked the shit out of each other in a corridor. It was not an auspicious start to such an enduring and productive partnership. The partnership began life as a juvenile dope-spoof inspired by Cheech & Chong called Los Faces. It would eventually bear sweeter fruit as the heart and soul of the Red Hot Chili Peppers.

"He (Kiedis) looked like a lunatic," said Michael Balzary. "I figured I'd better get on his good side. He had short little flat-top; he looked weird."

The liberal regime at Fairfax agreed with Kiedis and Balzary. The school had, in the past, produced such luminaries as Herb Alpert and Phil Spector. In 1958, past Fairfax scholars would spend a total of nine weeks at the top of the American charts.

Kiedis and Balzary had similar experiences at Fairfax. Both were initially loners. Kiedis had just one close friend – Tony Sherr. Balzary was the butt of endless cruel jokes in class due to his expertise on the trumpet and his teachers' subsequent admiration.

Michael Balzary was born in Melbourne, Western Australia, on October 16, 1962. He was 16 days older than Kiedis and, like Anthony, his parents divorced when he was a child. His mother (Patricia) re-married a New York City jazz musician (Walter Urban Jnr) in 1967, and took Michael (aged four) and his older sister to the Big Apple to live.

In contrast to Anthony Kiedis' teenage years spent investigating and savouring the pleasures of the flesh in Los Angeles, Michael Balzary's first love was a trumpet hand-made by Dominic Calicchio. By the age of eleven, when the family re-located to Los Angeles, Michael was already a child jazz boffin.

At the age of 14, Anthony Kiedis had won the part of Sylvester Stallone's son in the dumb re-working of Joe Eszterhas' movie based on the life of Unionist Johnny Kovak. F.I.S.T. was a turkey of a movie, a vehicle for Stallone's delusion of literary grandeur and little else.

F.I.S.T. is generously described in Steven Scheuer's Movies On TV as "overlong but engrossing". It makes no mention of Kiedis (acting under the name Cole Dammett) and, according to one of Kiedis' Fairfax classmates: "Anthony was an actor, but Anthony was an actor in the school play! I didn't even remember the movie until he started discussing it interviews half a decade later."

But it was nonetheless another story in Anthony Kiedis' ever-expanding collection.

> *"It was the greatest thing in the world to have all these beautiful women come into my house and not be uptight about me hanging out with them."*

At the same age, Michael Balzary admitted that "the most exciting fucking thing in my life" was meeting Dizzy Gillespie, and being held in the great jazz man's arms right up until he went on-stage.

Michael's love for music was pure and untainted. Eschewing the burgeoning punk and glam scene in LA, he would instead perfect his trumpet technique alone in his bedroom. Sometimes he would even be invited to join Walter Urban's freeform jazz jams.

Michael Balzary, as a nerdy teenager, was as cool as porridge.
Anthony Kiedis, as a precocious Valentino and loud-mouthed high roller, was a pain in the ass.

But without each other at Fairfax, Anthony Kiedis would not have had anyone to corrupt, and Michael Balzary would not have become Mike B the Flea. The two became inseparable. Pretty soon they were notorious.

There would be no Red Hot Chili Peppers without a band formed by two fully paid-up soldiers in the Kiss Army. Jack Irons and Hillel Slovak were utter Kiss addicts and slaves to possibly the crappest band in the world. Bonded by face paint and stacked heels, the pair took their obsession to its logical conclusion and formed a copycat stage act of their cartoon heroes.

"Hillel would be Paul Stanley," says Fairfax classmate and friend Alain Johannes, "Jack was Gene Simmons. They built their own Kiss costumes, Jack got some frothing blood capsules, and they'd put on these shows in class, where they mimed to the records. They used to stay up all night doing their make-up for the shows."

Hillel and Jack were both Jewish, although the latter was a native Californian. Hillel had been born in Haifa, Israel, but had re-located to Los Angeles at the age of five. The two met within the city's tight-knit Jewish community and were already close friends when they entered Fairfax.

Jack Irons only knew one thing for certain – that he was going to beat the shit out of a drumkit for his living. Hillel Slovak, on the other hand, would lie in his bedroom and weep for Hendrix's soul and abandon. He was taking formal lessons (as was Jack Irons), but Bert Weedon was no substitute for 'All Along The Watchtower' or 'Foxy Lady'.

Anthony Kiedis described Hillel Slovak at Fairfax as "a kind of funny-looking kid, real skinny with long hair and big lips".

Jack Irons' and Hillel Slovak's Fairfax photographs make them look like girls. Both look fresh-faced and almost cherubic.

When Jack and Hillel eventually became Chili Peppers, nobody remembered very much about Anthem – the High School band assembled by Alain Johannes in 1977 featuring Irons (drums), Slovak (guitar), Todd Strasman (bass) and a repertoire of songs relying heavily on Kiss, Queen and Led Zeppelin. It was a middle-class sound, untouched by the rush of punk or the hammer-fist of hardcore raging out there beyond the safe Fairfax campus.

"I was a late bloomer to the whole concept of punk," Jack Irons would later admit with admirable honesty. "I wasn't a rebel when I was a teenager. I was kinda happy, so I don't think I actually understood what the music meant, as opposed to what it sounded like. It was too crazy. I didn't understand that there was a reason for that craziness."

Instead Anthem would persevere with a song based on Queen's sprawling 'Ogre Battle'. They would bum the high notes and squash the intended moodscape into a flabby puddle of AOR.

Like every school band in the world, Anthem were awkward, clichéd and pretentious. They rehearsed at Jack Irons' long-suffering parents' house every day after school, studiously perfecting their plod rock chops and dreaming about their second gig. Today Anthem sound as awful as Canned Heat in short trousers.

Meanwhile, Anthony Kiedis and Mike B the Flea were attempting to pogo off this mortal coil with a bong and a hard-on.

"I wasn't a rebel when I was a teenager. I was kinda happy, so I don't think I actually understood what the music meant, as opposed to what it sounded like. It was too crazy. I didn't understand that there was a reason for that craziness."

Alain Johannes recalls the Fairfax exploits of Mike B and Anthony Kiedis.

"They really did have little angels looking out for them."

Like the time they scaled a giant billboard on Melrose and waved their dicks at the assembled onlookers below. Like the time they took off for a 48-hour skiing trip and slept in a launderette to keep warm. Like the times Anthony hurtled through the LA road grids in a neat little car with no brakes. He never hit a thing. Like the time he dived into an empty swimming and fractured his back.

"Another friend ran away," says Anthony, "but Flea stayed, dealt with the cops, and made sure I got to hospital."

"Two weeks later," says Alain Johannes, "he was walking around as though nothing had happened, with just this little support thing. Those two used to get themselves into terrible trouble."

1980 was graduation year for Anthony, Flea, Jack Irons, Alain Johannes and Hillel Slovak. It was the summer before the great unknown – out there somewhere beyond the accommodating Fairfax cheerleaders (Anthony was then dating a cheerleader called Haya Handel), the endless keg parties on the beach, and the group's bold experiments with mild hallucinogenics. Back then it was just a group of friends trying to get a kick out of anything. It wasn't a big deal.

Anthony: "When Hillel and I were kids, and Flea also, we were heavy-duty drug experimenters. We took LSD, we did cocaine, we did heroin, smoked a lot of pot and did a lot of alcohol and different combinations of barbiturates. But it was all in good fun. We weren't slaves to the drugs."

They were fuelled by teenage bravado. Life was a breeze – a cool Californian breeze that can so easily dull the harsh realities of real life. They were buddies looking for another high, another orifice, another heartbeat. Life was pretty sweet for Los Faces.

At the centre of their social whirlpool, Alain Johannes' Anthem acted as a catalyst.

The name had been changed to Anthym following pressure from another, more established local band with the same name. Bassist Todd Strasman had quit in favour of law school. His natural replacement was Anthony Kiedis' wild-eyed tearaway partner.

Mike B the Flea picked up a bass guitar and knew instinctively what to do with the four thick strings. He had just one formal lesson but walked out after the hippy teacher offered him a copy of The Eagles' 'Take It Easy' as homework. "I decided just to figure stuff out on my own," he says.

Gradually, Anthym began to lose the fussy plod metal floss and evolve into a near-credible Hollywood attraction. Despite the age of the group, and subsequent problems with promoters worried about their clubs' age restrictions, the band rolled out onto the tough local circuit with a cocky confidence born more of ignorance than experience. It was a tough initiation.

Anthym were badly bottled by neo-Nazis when they supported Oingo Boingo at the Orange County Fair. Alain and Hillel received bruises, but they at least escaped intact. Such incidences, however, were outweighed by their regular headline at the Starwood club's Young Nights package.

"We did manage to create quite a little following," Johannes remembers. "We could play the Troubadour and pack it, then go back to school on Monday and feel like we were stars. And of course our grades started to plummet because we got all cocky about it."

18

Although Alain Johannes – as principal song-smith – was undoubtedly Anthym's master, it was Hillel and Flea who spurred the band into deeper and bolder pastures. Alain was an accomplished guitarist, yet he was an old school plodder who never fully embraced the brutal LA hardcore scene that so excited Hillel, Flea, and particularly Anthony Kiedis.

"I was heavily into jazz at this point," Alain Johannes says. "I didn't really know much about punk. There was a whole group of kids who were into that stuff a lot more than we were; we were still into Led Zeppelin and Stevie Wonder and so on."

"We could play the Troubadour and pack it, then go back to school on Monday and feel like we were stars. And of course our grades started to plummet because we got all cocky about it."

The unlikeliest convert to the scene was Flea. Anthym's bass player was a hardcore virgin until he saw Black Flag play their first ever gig with new frontman Henry Rollins at the LA Starwood club.

At the time, Flea remembers thinking that the experience was "disgusting". Yet Hillel and Anthony raged through the scene with such passion that Flea saw the light. He took the time to understand the fierce pride of hardcore, the furious commitment to carving a life out of the garbage, of straining every sinew in your efforts to better yourself and achieve something from nothing. Flea was inspired.

"What punk rock was about to me," he later explained, "was never having to say you're sorry."

So Flea and Anthony never apologised to anyone for hitching a ride down to San Francisco to get mohawked. On the way back they got a ride from a man with 'Los Venos Chicos' tattooed on his neck. When they arrived in LA, the driver gave Flea and Anthony the car.

"I stole it!" he told them, and ran off.

The haircut got Flea fired from the animal hospital where he worked after graduating. But hardcore was never having to apologise, and Flea wasn't sorry. The newly-shaved bassist was developing not only as a player but also as a showman, and developing at an alarming rate.

His stage antics were exuberant. He alone made Anthym an entertaining proposition. His bass playing was sophisticated, ruthless, and totally hardcore. Anthym's music became more intricate as a result, prompting Anthony Kiedis to conceive a new moniker: What Is This? Anthym, everyone agreed, sounded like another run-of-the-mill, poodle-permed heavy metal troupe posing along Sunset Strip.

Kiedis himself had remained the band's most vocal supporter. He had even become their unofficial MC, delivering a scripted introduction before stage-diving into the crowd to slam dance his way through the crowd alongside Haya.

"Cal Worthington calls them the hottest rockers in LA!" he would bawl. "Their parents call them crazy and the girls call them all the time...!"

But Flea knew in his heart that What Is This? was going nowhere.

The Los Faces graduated from Fairfax in 1980 and were not expected to achieve anything. Anthony, Hillel, Jack, Alain and Flea's constant search for exciting diversions at Fairfax had not left a great impression on the High School's teaching body, and the average grades they consequently received were hardly a great advertisement.

Surprisingly, it was only Anthony Kiedis who opted willingly for further education. He credits his father and "several exceptional teachers" for nurturing his love of writing and poetry, and after his graduation summer he enrolled at UCLA at the age of 18.

Only Flea and Hillel decided to make a stab at a career in music, whilst Jack Irons and Alain Johannes both enrolled in feeble Californian colleges as a means of prolonging the agony of standing up on two feet.

After almost three years, Anthony and Haya Handel had finally parted. Anthony endured less than one year at UCLA before dropping out to start work as a clerk in a small Hollywood film studio. He still held on to his aspirations of somehow making it as an actor. It was a dull job, and an existence that seemed somehow futile. To compensate, he embarked on what he today describes as "a crash course in low-brow gluttony. My sex life was happy and I was rocking!"

Blackie had become less of an inspiration to Anthony Kiedis Jnr was 19 and working his way through a succession of willing partners, experimenting with any substance (chemical and physical) to kill the boredom of nine-to-five.

21

Anthony was still at the centre of What Is This?'s social whirl. It was this scene, as well as a low boredom threshold, which began to drag both Anthony and Hillel deeper into the comforting drug culture of Hollywood. The pair's consumption had upped considerably from the halcyon days at Fairfax. It was not yet a problem, but a means to an end. Most mornings they woke up and couldn't even remember the drug they'd scored from some guy the night before. It took them a while even to remember the night before. By now, the night before had usually revolved around one of LA's seedy basement dives catering for a whole new clientele.

Anthony still wrote poetry for fun, borrowing heavily from the new underground rap scene that had, by now, snaked across the country from New York. He was an immediate convert to the DIY ethics of rap. Spiritually, if not musically, aligned to hardcore, rap was another cult soul protest. It was another great liberator, and so far untainted by the clammy saccharine hands of the mainstream pale faces. In 1981, Run DMC's giant crossover hit with Aerosmith's 'Walk This Way' was still five years away.

"Rap," Anthony later explained, "gave me the notion that I could do something musical without being Marvin Gaye!"

"Cal Worthington calls them the hottest rockers in LA!" he would bawl. "Their parents call them crazy and the girls call them all the time . . . !"

On 1st August, 1981, America received MTV between the eyes. Pop music mind control was here to stay. Music would never be as dangerous again, now that pop music had to provide a neat video snip to earn airplay and consequently keep the rednecks and liberals alike as happy as bland-boys out there in Nowheresville. That month, the US singles chart featured the likes of Rick Springfield ('Jessie's Girl'), Manhattan Transfer ('The Boy From New York City'), Foreigner ('Urgent') and the Alan Parsons Project ('Time').

The American mainstream was still fast asleep. It was hopelessly out of touch with the desires and hopes and lives of Anthony Kiedis and Flea as to be absolutely irrelevant. Neither teenager even owned a radio. Both had always preferred to discover their own music rather than be force-fed the radio diet of empty disco and trite soft rock. It was a healthy ignorance and disrespect for the mainstream media that even today marks the Red Hot Chili Peppers as an uncomfortable thrill.

22

By now Flea had temporarily abandoned What Is This? for something a little more challenging. When he heard on the grapevine that Fear were short of a bassist following the departure of Derf Scratch, he went to a gig and sold himself an audition.

Fear were old wave punks with a reputation for confrontation and liberal-baiting. Flea's sophisticated style of bass-abuse was not the most suitable, but Fear were constantly gigging and had a schedule to fulfil.

"Fear was the first band I was in that made any money and that people came to see," Flea recalls.

It was an uncomfortable experience. Fear tried to tame Flea's style – insisting he use a plectrum for the first time in his life – and consequently Flea tried to funk up Fear. The internal struggle would manifest itself as one of LA's most explosive live shows on the circuit. It was such an attraction that Flea was singled out by ex-Sex Pistol Johnny Rotten (now John Lydon) as a possible replacement for departed P.i.L bassist Jah Wobble.

Flea did audition for P.i.L but, according to drummer Martin Atkins, asked for a few days to consider the band's offer to tour Japan and Australia. Ultimately he declined.

Says Flea: "I thought about it, but ultimately I thought 'Fuck that, I'm not going to be a sideman for someone else'!"

Flea re-joined Fear in LA. He never recorded with the band but was featured as a band member in Penelope Spheeris' Suburbia movie – a heavy-handed attempt at capturing the sleaze and struggle of Los Angeles' burgeoning punk community.

A bit-part actress by the name of Alison Braun remembers Flea's character, Razzle. "He was given a rat to carry around. How... punk!"
The film was quite rightly a flop; a movie whose sole impressive feature was the speed at which it nose-dived forever into the bargain basement bins of video rental stores. Ironically, it took up residence alongside F.I.S.T. – Anthony Kiedis' first faltering steps onto the silver screen alongside Sly Stallone. Spheeris, however, went on to earn the respect of her peers with her horrifically entertaining series of low-budget docu-flicks entitled The Decline Of Western Civilization.

It was spring 1983 in Los Angeles. Nothing much was happening in the lives of either Anthony Kiedis, Flea, Hillel Slovak or Jack Irons. What Is This? continued to play averagely-attended club gigs around town. The only concrete thing on the horizon was an offer for Anthony Kiedis to put together a brief, one-off routine to open a show by Gary Allen at the Rhythm Lounge. The two knew of each other, but were hardly close friends. Gary Allen knew Anthony only as "a wild man who would do anything for a laugh!".

Flea and Anthony were lazily jamming in the latter's apartment. Flea was doodling on his bass when he tumbled across the thinnest of riffs. He repeated the riff for a while. Anthony started to rap some poetry he had jotted down following a show by Grandmaster Flash And The Furious Five the previous week. It was called 'Out In LA' Anthony and Flea guessed they had something there that could be used in the up-coming 'one-off' routine at the Rhythm Lounge.

As the first song ever written by something that would soon become the Red Hot Chili Peppers, 'Out In LA' wasn't great at all. But it would do.

Chapter 3

Flea remembers that "I had a bass line and Anthony had a poem". Tony Flow and The Miraculously Majestic Masters Of Mayhem each took a tab of acid and exploded into life for about four minutes.

As has already been noted, if anybody had popped out for a piss they would have missed the entire set.

Flea and Anthony had recruited Jack Irons and Hillel Slovak from What Is This? for one night only. They were simply the most obvious and under-committed friends available. No-one had bothered to rehearse. Rehearsals were for pussies.

They plugged in with the mischievous, cocky abandon of a band who were doing all this for a joke and didn't care who knew it and, shit, no-one was going to take it seriously with a name like that and, anyway, who gives a fuck? The Rhythm Lounge gave a fuck. Big time. Tony Flow and The Miraculously Majestic Masters Of Mayhem stunned the small crowd and were immediately offered a headline slot at the club if they could maybe write a few more songs. No-one was more amazed at the reaction than the four band members themselves.

Flea: "We played our first gig as a joke and the next time we played, there were lines around the block!"

Tony Flow and The Miraculously Majestic Masters Of Mayhem immediately disappeared. In their place the very next day – and inspired, Anthony Kiedis still insists, by a "psychedelic bush with band names on it" – stood the Red Hot Chili Peppers.

The Red Hot Chili Peppers? Spicy, zangy, substantial, nutty, Mexican, off the wall, dumb... the name was perfect. The Red Hot Chili Peppers were all these things and they had two whole fucking songs!

"We had 'Out In LA'," says Jack Irons, "and we added 'Get Up And Jump'. It wasn't like we were trying to fool anybody. We only had two songs and people wanted to come and see us, so that's all we could give them!"

The band were a joke. Yet Flea points out that it was never a pre-meditated joke.

"I never thought, 'hey, I've got a great idea! Let's take punk rock and funk and put them together and make a song!'. It was just elements of the things that I loved. It was never really conscious. I liked playing funk, but the natural me was very aggressive. I liked that feeling of beating the shit out of the bass, but doing it in a funky way."

27

"I never thought, 'hey, I've got a great idea! Let's take punk rock and funk and put them together and make a song!'. It was just elements of the things that I loved. It was never really conscious. I liked playing funk, but the natural me was very aggressive. I liked that feeling of beating the shit out of the bass, but doing it in a funky way."

It was also that very first gig which set a precedent for how the Red Hot Chili Peppers would continue to work throughout their career. The music would originate from Flea and be pumped full of life and shade by Slovak and Irons. Anthony Kiedis would scatter-rap his lyrics in a voice that would invigorate and entertain, but take years to mature fully and hold down a commercial tune.

Yet Kiedis, even back then at the Rhythm Lounge, was always the showman. An extraordinary showman with the balls and bravado to get away with it. The four were young, fit and giddy, and right now everybody seemed to think that there could be a future in this bizarre melting pot that had become the Red Hot Chili Peppers. They had nailed freaky-styley to the flagpole.

As the small club gigs began steadily to accelerate, so too did the lifestyle that went with it. And no-one in the Red Hot Chili Peppers was about to act as a voice of reason.

Chapter 4

The four friends shared an apartment. It was a free-spirited den where anything went and nothing really mattered. Girls would drop by, drop their knickers, and drop their guard. Dealers would drop in and drop out with the Red Hot Chili Peppers. A nearby grocery store would off-load a beer mountain during the summer of 1983.

The Chili Peppers would play anywhere in LA. They had developed something of a set – fusing their primal hardcore funk with lilting campfire songs, and usually encoring with Jimi Hendrix's 'Fire'. The crowds flocked to witness this exhilarating beast. Chaos would never be far away from a Red Hot Chili Peppers gig.

As Anthony Kiedis put it: "It was all a matter of us being friends, and what a fine idea it would be to have four close friends as bearers of the zany new funk we had in our minds and our bodies."

Flea: "It was really fun. We started to play more shows, and write more songs. Then all of a sudden people started to take us seriously, and lawyers started trying to get us record contracts and shit."

It was during these formative summer months that the Red Hot Chili Peppers performed a notorious stunt that would later overshadow much of their music. The Socks-On-Cocks routine was never meant to be that big a deal. Certainly it was never the sum total of the Chili Peppers' experience.

The Kit Kat club is a glitzy strip joint in Hollywood. LA has hundreds of strip bars. It's where the struggling actresses go to earn the rent money until the blockbuster movie deal is offered. The Kit Kat is flasher and tackier than most, in a time-warped '70s way. The girls would dance on pillars and on the stage whilst a band played. There was a strict house rule forbidding the display of a single pubic hair. So the girls would dance topless with just the flimsiest G-string covering their carefully-shaven bikini lines. Of course the Red Hot Chili Peppers wanted to play the Kit Kat club.

It was not a good gig. The band tried every stunt in the book to distract the audience's attention from the gyrating dancers. The Chili Peppers, they felt, were sexier than this on their own. They completed the set and sat backstage whilst the promoter insisted they return for an encore.

And then Flea remembered Anthony's sock.

While at UCLA Anthony had found himself the unwanted target of a girl he didn't fancy bedding. She was persistent. "She would send me these cards with fold-out cocks," he says, "with the yardstick on them!"

When the girl finally showed up at his apartment, in exasperation Anthony answered the door stark naked save for a sock over his cock. The girl fled. Backstage at the Kit Kat, the band considered this scenario for maybe a split second. Then they gleefully stripped and returned for their encore wearing just a sock over their manhoods.

"We were levitating with nervous energy," Anthony remembers. "I could not find my feet on stage. And somebody filmed it. I don't know if the film still exists (it doesn't), but we saw it, and we just had this look in our eyes like we were from outer space."

Jack Irons laughs at the memory. "That was one of the fucking funniest moments of my life! It was so funny I started to pee in my sock.

"But it was that simple, it was us trying to upstage the strippers who were dancing in their G-strings next to us.

The promoter was waiting for them after the show. "No pubes!" he allegedly screamed. "I told you guys no pubes!"

"It was really fun. We started to play more shows, and write more songs. Then all of a sudden people started to take us seriously, and lawyers started trying to get us record contracts and shit."

It was a good stunt. It was used, according to Lindy Goetz (who was in the Kit Kat that night and went on to manage the band) during maybe only "15% of all the gigs the band ever played", but for years remained the Red Hot Chili Peppers' best remembered antic.

It even caught on at the apartment they all shared. As Flea says: "Friends would drop by to hang out, smoke pot and drink beer, and sooner or later we'd put socks on our dicks and run around. It was kids living together, having fun. That's all."

Such antics earned the Red Hot Chili Peppers a reputation, and reputations sell records. No-one could seriously believe that just six months after forming as a one-off joke, the Red Hot Chili Peppers were being courted by the major record labels in Los Angeles.

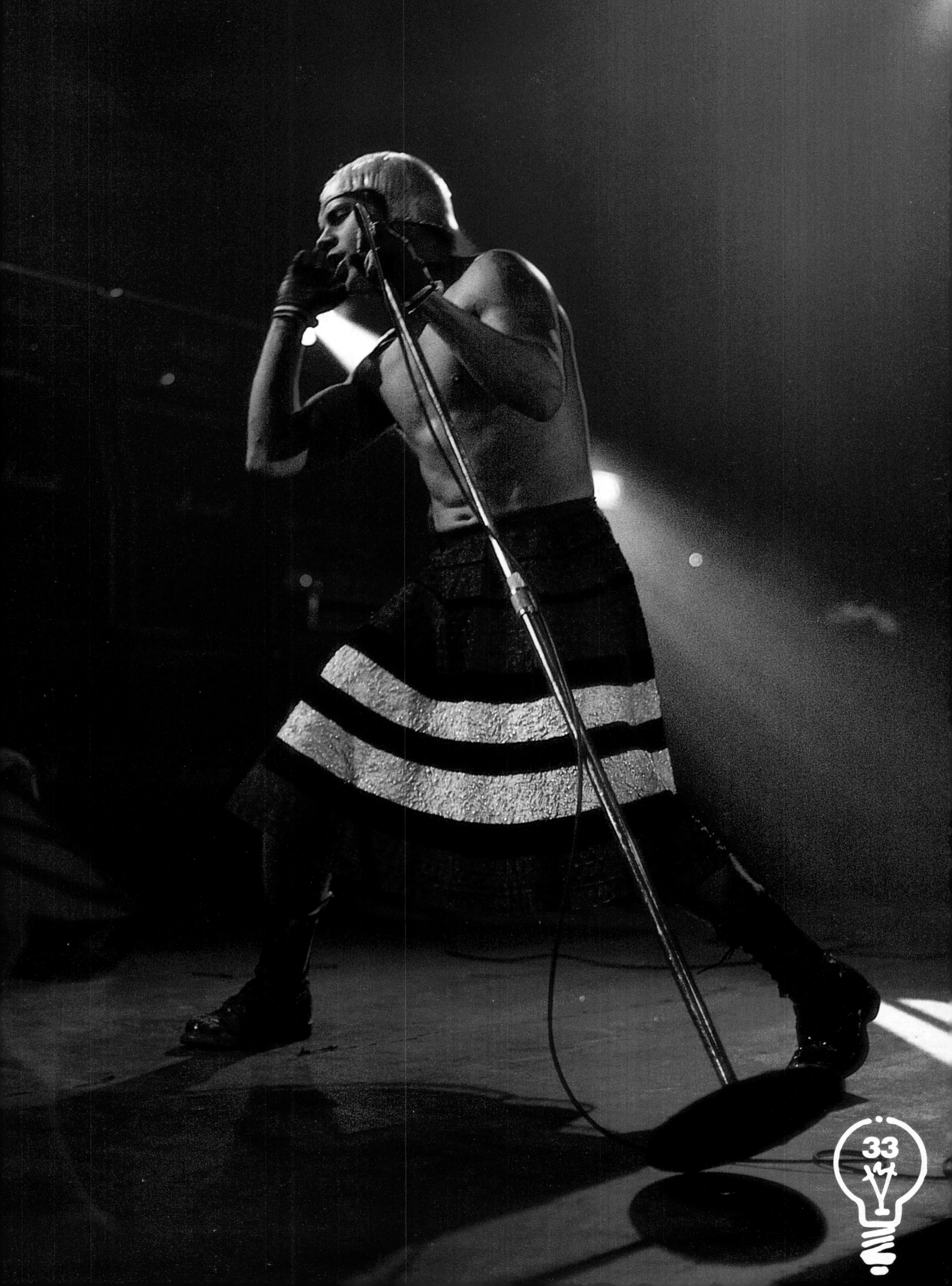

Mark 'Rooster' Richardson was a freelance studio engineer working out of Atlanta, Georgia. A sharp brain, a keen ear and a fast mouth meant that he had gravitated towards the centre of every rising scene in America and Britain since the mid-'70s. He had witnessed the rise of such East Coast scenesters as Patti Smith and The Ramones in 1976, as well as the explosive London scene a year later. Rooster was on the West Coast towards the end of the decade, smashing around in the hardcore maelstrom and picking his way through the jungle of underground funk clubs.

Rooster was anti-mainstream, anti-Establishment, and anti-celebrity. It was perfectly natural that he should eventually stumble across the Red Hot Chili Peppers' experience. He had actually heard about the band from a Hollywood director who had worked in the past with Anthony's father, Blackie Dammett. Rooster Richardson was immediately blown away by the sheer frenzy, fury and fun of these giant mohawked magpies.

The sound was a mess. The audience, however – predominantly W.A.S.P. Lolitas and a smattering of bull-faced punks – didn't care. It was a typical Red Hot Chili Peppers gig and Rooster Richardson wasted little time on formal introductions. Within days of meeting, the band were booked into Bijou studios to cut their first ever demo tape.

They worked fast, keener to capture the vibe of the live show than any individual musical virtuosity. It was the way the band would always try and work on subsequent sessions. It was the way Rooster had always worked. As a result, the five songs they recorded (the two very first songs Anthony and Flea wrote together – 'Out In LA' and 'Get Up And Jump' – as well as 'Green Heaven', 'Sex Rap' and 'Baby Appeal') stood out from the stack of soft rock cassettes cluttering up the A&R offices of the major labels.

It was a new sound. A whole new thing for the major labels to try and understand. The sound, they knew from their talent scouts out there on the streets, was popular. It was the next big thing. Honest. Trust us on this one. Go with it. That was really all the major record labels needed to know. There was a market for the Red Hot Chili Peppers. Quite how to tap into and exploit that market would be a whole new headache. The Red Hot Chili Peppers hoped that the record companies would hate the tape.

EMI Records in Los Angeles were immediately enthusiastic. Rooster Richardson was in overdrive, hammering home the point of the Red Hot Chili Peppers to a boardroom full of fat executives still celebrating the success of David Bowie's 'Let's Dance' album. Other major labels heard on the grapevine that EMI were interested, and consequently dispatched teams of brown-nosing, coke-addled executives to woo the band into that particular hall of fame.

EMI were not offering the most lucrative deal on the table, but because they had been the first company to show an active interest, the Red Hot Chili Peppers decided to accept a contract and hope for the best. It had been barely six months since Tony Flow and The Miraculously Majestic Masters Of Mayhem had played just one song at the Rhythm Lounge. Now here they were, captive major label protegés with the chance to achieve something from nothing. It was not be so simple.

The red Hot Chili Peppers were signed to EMI America as a full band complete with all the usual things a major label might not unreasonably expect: a stable line-up, a debut album's worth of material and a natural urge to co-operate. If that was the case then EMI quickly discovered that they had signed the wrong band.

The Red Hot Chili Peppers were not actually a proper band at all. It was a vehicle for Flea and Anthony to show off at parties, aided and abetted by Jack Irons and Hillel Slovak who were both still very much an integral part of Alain Johannes' What Is This?. Flea was still officially a member of Fear, although he never claimed to be anything other than a hired hand. In signing the Red Hot Chili Peppers, EMI could only really be certain of securing the services of Anthony Kiedis and Flea. Right up until work began on what would be the band's debut album, Irons and Slovak were caught in a dilemma that centred around their loyalty to Alain Johannes. The Red Hot Chili Peppers, the drummer and guitarist had always been led to believe, was good fun and an excuse to indulge. The fact that the 'joke' had been signed to a major label didn't mean that the Chili Peppers were about to offer the pair a more stable existence. Except that no-one – not even Rooster and the man he had recruited to manage the band, Lindy Goetz – had told EMI.

For a while, there was a great deal of confusion in Los Angeles. Ultimately it took another major label to force the Red Hot Chili Peppers' hand. Rather, the company (MCA) forced Jack Irons and Hillel Slovak to resolve the dilemma.

Inspired by EMI's interest in the Red Hot Chili Peppers, and sure that the band was now certain to sign the deal, MCA had begun to scour Los Angeles for something similar. It didn't take them long to find What Is This?. Although What Is This? played a more intricate and decidedly more high-brow variation on the Chili's rap punk fusion, they appeared to be sufficiently close to EMI's blueprint to fit the description. This was hardly surprising, since What Is This? boasted the Red Hot Chili Peppers' guitarist and drummer!

Jack Irons and Hillel Slovak couldn't understand all the fuss. For a while they seriously intended to work with both bands, dismissing allegations of a conflict of interest as mere corporate paranoia. But there was also pressure from Alain Johannes, who told Jack and Hillel that the situation would indeed be "unworkable".

REDHOTCHILIPEPPERS
SUGARANDSPICE

REDHOTCHILIPEPPERS
SUGARANDSPICE

It was a blow to both Flea and Anthony Kiedis when Hillel and Jack finally decided to stay with the devil they had known since Fairfax High School. For the time being at least, What Is This? looked a decidedly stronger bet. The ink had not even dried on their EMI contract, and already the Red Hot Chili Peppers were in disarray.

Anthony later admitted that he went home and cried.

"I was emotionally devastated. I was so happy finally to be in a band and strutting my stuff around town, and for my friends to fall out like that... I thought we were over."

Flea put on a braver face. "What were they (Jack and Hillel) supposed to do: go with the joke band that got a deal after six months? Or with the band they dedicated themselves to for six years? They went with What Is This?, which is completely understandable."

Flea's voice of sanity rung out like a bell, but it didn't help his and Anthony's problems. EMI were far from happy at the situation and gave what was left of the Red Hot Chili Peppers just two months to secure the services of a reliable drummer and guitarist. The company wanted the band in the studio as quickly as possible, hoping to pip MCA to the product release post. EMI would fail, but the Red Hot Chili Peppers did indeed make it into the recording studio with a new drummer and guitarist.

It was a worst case scenario for Kiedis and Flea. Held over a barrel by a major recording label and having to secure two people who could fill the shoes of exceptionally close friends. It was impossible. Ultimately it was a situation that hampered the Red Hot Chili Peppers' career for two years.

Jack Sherman was an accomplished session guitarist who was able to accommodate almost any musical style with flair and soul. Cliff Martinez was a friend of Flea and had been the drummer in Lydia Lunch's ill-fated 13.13 project. Both received a crash-course in the Chili Pepper psyche and were told to get on with it. "What we originally set out to do," says Anthony, "was to be complete and utter perpetrators of hardcore, bone-crunching mayhem sex things from heaven. To try and describe that to another musician, and have it mean something, is nearly impossible unless you've grown up with that person.

"It was crazy, but when you get a guy in the band you've got to be prepared to embrace him emotionally for years and years. It's very much like being in love and being married. And you have to be willing to accept and tolerate and compromise sometimes."

Jack and Cliff shrugged and got on with it. But the resulting album – compared to the band's later output – was proof that you can't fake a Red Hot Chili Pepper.

38

Chapter 5

nthony Kiedis wanted to call the first Red Hot Chili Peppers' record 'True Men Don't Kill Coyotes'. EMI absolutely did not. Producer Andy Gill just wanted to go home. The whole fucking thing had been a frazzling experience for everybody concerned.

The corporate EMI hierarchy reckoned that the Gang Of Four's Andy Gill was an ideal producer for the Red Hot Chili Peppers. Gang Of Four, although splintering despite signs of a commercial breakthrough in North America at the same time as the Chili Peppers were signing their deal, were also on the same label in the UK. Hence there were few logistical problems. Andy Gill and the Red Hot Chili Peppers also shared similar political views, albeit on totally different cultures. On paper at least, the partnership seemed to be the one to capture the frenzy of the Chili Peppers' live show.

But neither EMI nor the Red Hot Chili Peppers had bargained for the effect of being locked in a studio with the off-hand and technically-minded limey. To Flea and Anthony Kiedis, Andy Gill was a brain surgeon and their music needed a witch doctor.

"Maybe he (Gill) was just too English for us!" Flea later acknowledged.
"We knew what we wanted. We wanted a raw fucking rocking album. We didn't get it. I really regret our inability to deal with Andy Gill."

The recording sessions, although productive, were always a two-way battle between the experience of their producer and the band's sheer exuberance. Jack Irons, Hillel Slovak and Alain Johannes would all pop into the studio to lend encouragement, but the album was constructed on two entirely different wavelengths. The situation escalated into outright provocation.

It had been a long session. Anthony and Flea decided to liven up the proceedings. They told Andy Gill they were going to visit the bathroom. "Yeah," Gill replied, "don't trouble me by bringing it back, right?"

Anthony: "So Flea and I went and took the shit out of the toilet, brought it back in a pizza box, and we gave it Andy. All he could say was 'typical'!"

Although he laboured far beyond the call of duty to supply EMI with a hit record, Andy Gill did not get along with the two main Peppers at all. The atmosphere was strained and the resulting album was a pale imitation of the Red Hot Chili Peppers.

Flea: "Basically, we ended up with a record stuck in between."

"We knew what we wanted. We wanted a raw fucking rocking album. We didn't get it. I really regret our inability to deal with Andy Gill."

EMI called the album 'The Red Hot Chili Peppers'. Wow! Despite diluting the likes of 'Out In LA' and 'Get Up And Jump' with what Kiedis and Flea later referred to as "namby-pampy-synth-pop", the album could boast at least the occasional burst of genuine Chili Peppers' magic. 'True Men Don't Kill Coyotes' remains the album's sucker punch; a blitzkrieg rap rant on the recent spate of wild animal shootings in the Hollywood hills. Another is the multi-mood instrumental, 'Grand Pappy Du Plenty', which hinted at a musical proficiency and diversity hitherto missing from the equation.

Yet it was an awkward record.

"We didn't have the groove at the time," says Flea. "We had Cliff and Jack, and I don't think that configuration was capable of creating a groove."

It was 1984 and it was not a good year for the Red Hot Chili Peppers. The economic yuppy boom had arrived and everyone was looking out for No.1. 1984 was all about Lionel Richie, Frankie Goes To Hollywood, Culture Club, Michael Jackson and Band/Live Aid. 1984 was not about the debut album from half a bunch of upstart hardcore brats with socks on their cocks. So the Red Hot Chili Peppers embarked on their very first tour of America instead. If Mohammed won't go to the mountain, then the mountain must go to Mohammed. Or, in this case, the mountain must go to Illinois.

"My mom loves the socks!" said Anthony Kiedis.

REDHOTCHILIPEPP
SUGARANDSPICE

Chapter 6

No-one knew for sure exactly when Anthony Kiedis and Hillel Slovak became addicted to heroin. What had started as a teenage experiment at Fairfax had by now escalated to darker levels. Like most drug addicts, Anthony and Hillel had gradually increased their intake in order to get the same buzz. Over the course of two years they had become addicted. Anthony and Hillel were hooked.

Yet they were also supremely creative. Jack Irons had always been a staunch abstainer. Flea admits to having dabbled, but never to any great depth. Anthony and Hillel, however, were being drawn further and further into the underbelly of Los Angeles' heroin subculture. Together, as addicts, they were inseparable. As Anthony says today: "The more time passed, the more Hillel and I began to isolate. As kids, we considered those mind-expanding situations as a way to view life in a different way. Then eventually time passes and you either become an addict or you don't. We did. We needed that extra comfort."

As the Red Hot Chili Peppers began to tour the country, and as What Is This? were bobbing on the critical acclaim heaped upon their debut 'Squeezed' EP, so the addictions began to interfere with the creative process. Heroin was a pressure valve. It was also fun. But heroin was also a time-consuming addiction.

It was perhaps inevitable that two close friends in separate but similarly-aligned bands would eventually come together under one roof. It was no secret that the Red Hot Chili Peppers' tour had highlighted the band's shaky foundations. In the words of Jack Irons, Flea and Anthony "just did not like Jack Sherman".

Jack Sherman was just not cut out to be a fully-fledged Chili Pepper. When the band came off the road at the end of 1984, Flea and Anthony broke the news to Sherman that he was out of the band. At that time they had not secured a replacement. Anthony, however, knew exactly who to approach.

Hillel Slovak abandoned What Is This? in January 1985 to take up his rightful place beside Flea and Anthony in the Red Hot Chili Peppers. Nobody was particularly surprised.

"I knew in my head that it was inevitable Hillel would eventually go off with the others," says Jack Irons. "He and I both loved the Red Hot Chili Peppers; it was just that I had managed to erase them from my mind a little bit better than he had. He enjoyed playing that funky kind of thing. The album sessions (for the debut MCA record) suggested that What Is This? was developing into a very different kind of band. We'd been together a long time. He just wanted the chance to do something else."

And so Hillel Slovak was re-united with Anthony Kiedis and Flea. For the time being they were happy with Cliff Martinez. And Anthony was happy to have a junkie as a co-conspirator. It was time to go to work.

Anthony Kiedis and Hillel Slovak would score on the streets of Los Angeles. Anywhere. Even in the dangerous gang neighbourhoods of South Central; the dark boulevards and run-down alleys that even the locals walk on past without staring too hard at the deals going down. It didn't pay to get involved. It didn't pay to get noticed. Down there life just went on without you and that was the best way.

"I was just kind of hanging out on the streets and doing my thing," Anthony would later tell Rolling Stone magazine's David Fricke.

"I ran into some fairly unscrupulous characters involved with miniature Mafioso drug rings, and the hangout for one of these gangs was this particular location under a bridge. I ended up going there with this drug member, and the only way that I was allowed to go under this bridge was for him to tell everybody else that I was getting married to his sister. You had to be family to go there.

"That was one of just hundreds of predicaments that I found myself in, the kind that only drug addiction can bring about. It's not that that one place was more insidious than other places. But that's just one day that sticks very vividly in my memory. Like, how could I let myself get to that point?"

There was a time when Anthony half-heartedly enrolled for a session in Alcoholics Anonymous. He asked Hillel Slovak to come along for support and information.

"Why?" Hillel replied. "I'm not an alcoholic."

Hillel would never discuss his sources to the other three members of the Red Hot Chili Peppers. It was a typical act of denial. In not discussing his expanding consumption, and subsequently not volunteering to share his problem, Hillel could pretend that there was no problem. The more naturally extrovert Kiedis, however, made no secret of his addiction.

"Hillel thought he had power over the dark side," Anthony remembers today.

One local musician from an old hat of a bar band remembers the Red Hot Chili Peppers whilst they were working on their second album with George Clinton.

"Who was George Clinton in 1985, man? And who were the Red Hot Chili Peppers? It was a has-been hippy working with a bunch of never-will punks, and they behaved like they owned the city. Those guys were just out of control.

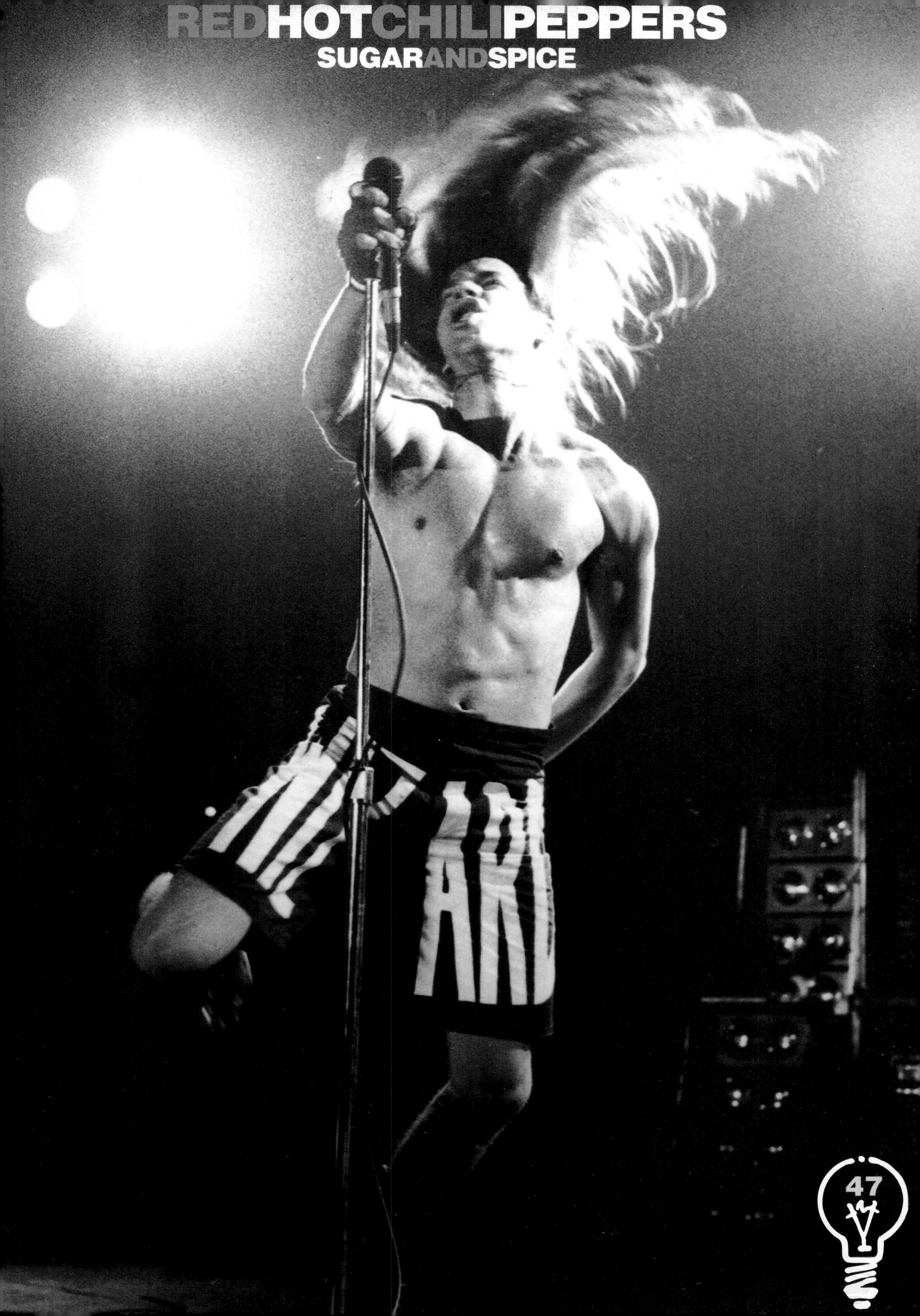

When other bands dropped in from out of town, the only thing they wanted to do was get up and jam. But the Peppers thought they were a big deal because they were from LA, because they were recording out in the sticks with George Clinton – who cares, man?"

The Red Hot Chili Peppers' first album had disappeared without a ripple. They had written enough material on tour to fill a second. Anthony and Flea had discovered and devoured such classic Funkadelic albums as 'Hardcore Jollies' and 'America Eats Its Young'.

"George Clinton is just amazing," Anthony would rave. "He's the ultimate hardcore funk creator in the world, ever. If anybody ever wanted to ask you what was the greatest funk metal ever, it would be Parliament-Funkadelic. Their music is so great that I don't think people are even capable of understanding how great it is."

In 1985, George Clinton was a recovering drug addict and a mellow, super-cool funk authority figure. His career had been iced by contractual problems with both Warner Brothers and Polygram, but this did not mean that he could not produce an album by these four enthusiastic and hyperactive acolytes.

EMI eagerly rubber-stamped the band's desire to work with Clinton in Detroit. The band insisted that they temporarily relocate to George Clinton's United Sound Studio in order to avoid the distractions of Los Angeles.

Compared to the infinitely stiffer-upper-lipped Andy Gill, anything should be an improvement. The early sessions could indeed boast a more coherent and focussed energy. But the idyllic surroundings of George Clinton's farm and his easy-going lifestyle soon began to drive the Red Hot Chili Peppers up the wall. The grand-daddy of funk metal had to instill at least a vestige of discipline into these four rubber balls. No matter how hard George Clinton tried to capture the music of the Red Hot Chili Peppers – and no matter how lurid and accomplished the results – the band were still principally a live band and unfamiliar with the possibilities of the studio.

The Red Hot Chili Peppers would labour all day to sweat their souls out onto tape. Clinton would be there behind the desk, a benevolent bear-man with a huge smile and an easy-going attitude. In the evening George Clinton would go fishing in his well-stocked pond in order to catch the follow morning's breakfast. For a while, even Anthony accompanied Clinton with rods, bait and tackle. After a while, however, the bright lights of Motor City presented a more attractive proposition.

As a team they would hit the town looking for action and inspiration. They were soon notorious in the bars and lounges of Detroit. As several bar bands pointed out, the Red Hot Chili Peppers were not always welcome.

49

Their natural enthusiasm could antagonise the slower, warier folk of Detroit. To them, this multi-coloured collection of loud-mouthed, street-sussed, smart-arsed barflies had done nothing and seemed highly likely to achieve less.

The Red Hot Chili Peppers, however, had good reason to be cocky. They were recording their second album for a major label. They were learning their craft at the feet of an old master. They had been re-united with Hillel Slovak and the machine was sounding suitably thick and oiled. Detroit could go take a hike.

Anthony Kiedis describes George Clinton in glowing terms. "He's just a bottomless pit of funky creativity who I have a great deal of respect for. I'm so fortunate to have had that experience of making a record with him. It's something that I'll never forget, and I'll always cherish it just as a blessing. It was a blessing to be able to hang out with him and to learn from him and to be a whole part of his feeling there."

"George Clinton is just amazing, he's the ultimate hardcore funk creator in the world, ever. If anybody ever wanted to ask you what was the greatest funk metal ever, it would be Parliament-Funkadelic. Their music is so great that I don't think people are even capable of understanding how great it is."

The Red Hot Chili Peppers had been founded on the bond between Anthony Kiedis and Flea. Hillel Slovak had been an honorary member, but was now accepted as an equal; a brother. It was important to all three that their music should never, ever become as stale and rigid as the singles that they constantly saw scaling the American charts. The soul had to be there. The spirits had to be kind, because only then could Hillel, Flea and Anthony conjure the monster. Music had to be an event rather than a mere career.

In many ways, 'Freaky Styley' would be regarded in retrospect as the Red Hot Chili Peppers' finest. The marriage between George Clinton and the band had paid dividends. The producer had guided the band towards a less frantic sound with a solid funk backbone, had steered them away from throwaway scatter-raps and into more rainbow pastures. It had not always been an easy process.

50

George Clinton demanded the most from Flea. He demanded that the bassist lean into his instrument and think of the sound as a muscle. Flea would be constantly interrupted by George Clinton's voice through his headphones. "If anybody else had done that to me," Flea says, "I'd be screaming 'shut the fuck up! I'm trying to play!'. But George Clinton could get away with it. Just." 'Freaky Styley' would also be the Chili Peppers' most overtly sexual document. Kiedis had grown in confidence as a lyricist and had naturally infused the songs with his own lurid sexual charms. The Red Hot Chili Peppers felt horny, and saw nothing wrong in documenting this fact.

'Sex Rap', then, was a showboating fuck serenade. 'Catholic School Girls Rule' – as the title suggests – echoed the fraternity environment at Fairfax and the apartment in which all four Chili Peppers would run around with socks on their cocks. Like, huh-huh-huh...

"Listen," Anthony Kiedis would later tell What's On magazine in 1991, "if people are true fans of the Red Hot Chili Peppers, then they know that we are not about sexism. The fact that there is a supremely potent sexual energy in our music is the most natural thing in the world for us and we don't feel any need to curtail that."

"We're not afraid to express our feelings, and if they're sexual feelings towards women, then they should be there in the music. It's very one-dimensional of these people to think that this is the sole basis of what we say and what we play. It's only one element. If that's all they can relate to, then maybe their minds are in the gutter."

EMI knew that this "supremely potent sexual energy" was a sure fire winner. The company was not entirely blameless in the consequent marketing strategy.

Anthony Kiedis had been inspired by the Live Aid shows to write a bitter attack on what he considered to be an overdose of celebrity guilt. 'Millionaires Against Hunger' never made it on to 'Freaky Styley'. Instead, EMI fell back on the duller choice of two cover versions (Sly Stone's 'If You Want Me To Stay' and The Meters' 'Africa' – cheekily retitled 'Hollywood'!), thus denying the band an opportunity to refute the claims of sexism through example. ('Millionaires Against Hunger' would later see the light of day on the B-side of the 'Taste The Pain' EP, whilst 'Hollywood' would be the first single taken from the album.)

The same fate had befallen a song on the band's debut album entitled 'Police Helicopter'. It was no more than a cartoon social comment on the LAPD's increasing use of surveillance helicopters at night, but it was still buried on 'The Red Hot Chili Peppers' beneath the more mental delights of 'Get Up And Jump' and 'Out In LA'.

The Red Hot Chili Peppers are proud to have occasionally over-stepped the boundaries of taste. The video for 'Catholic School Girls Rule' – never released prior to the 'Positive Mental Octopus' compilation – featured Anthony-as-Christ dragging a crucifix through a class of scantily-clad schoolgirls. In that same song, the line "let me see how deep, how deep is your throat" would haunt the band for some years to come.

"I would hope it's obvious that the Red Hot Chili Peppers aren't going to write lyrics that aren't explicit," Anthony told Sky magazine some years later, "because then we'd be a bunch of vague bastards!
"Our point is to get explicit within our lyrics, within our music, within our stage performance. The fact is, we'll never change what we feel and what we say to suit anybody's criteria.

"The cockmanship is secondary to the musicianship. If the cock has to flow then the cock has to flow. But you can't spend too much time worrying about that. What we have to say with our music is really what we're all about. The cock is just an added bonus.

"We're not afraid to express our feelings, and if they're sexual feelings towards women, then they should be there in the music. It's very one-dimensional of these people to think that this is the sole basis of what we say and what we play. It's only one element. If that's all they can relate to, then maybe their minds are in the gutter."

"We try put all aspects of our happiness, our sadness, our creative bursts of love, our creative bursts of hate, into our music. Being naked, having supreme sexual encounters, it's all part of our lives and it all gets funnelled into the sound. We don't have a straining net that catches the nudity and keeps it."

This is a typical Kiedis explanation; always the actor, the wordsmith and the hedonist. "Cockmanship" plays on Victorian values of valour and honour. He will always refer to the sexual act – of fucking a willing spiritual partner – in terms that neither denigrate nor humiliate that particular partner. Anthony Kiedis and the Red Hot Chili Peppers would always approach sex as the most utterly ordinary act between two consenting, healthy heterosexuals.

The Red Hot Chili Peppers have never rapped the praises of heavy metal sex. They have never dressed their conquests up in Mötley Crüe lingerie, there to be pawed and leered at by gruesome leather Himbos. They have never pretended to be in love, when love was just an excuse and a door to sex. The Red Hot Chili Peppers never pretended to be monks, and consequently wrote about it as they saw it. It was what they knew, as pretty fit 22-year-old men with the world at their feet. Even the Socks-On-Cocks routine was originally instigated to upstage strippers – never to compete with the dancers on some laddish ritual. As Anthony Kiedis told Details magazine in 1992: "We would get in our blue Chevy van and travel from town to town, and fate would see it straight, I would sample the local delicacies of the land. We had no pompous pretensions of 'You should fuck me because I'm in a rock'n'roll band'. It was more like 'You're here, I'm here... let's make each other happy right now'."

It was these explosions of rigorous sexual enthusiasm alone that would dog the Red Hot Chili Peppers as misogynist rapemen let loose to terrorise the Catholic virgins at the Central School of American Morality.

Unfortunately the band would later have the court writs to prove it.

Chapter 7

The Red Hot Chili Peppers took to the road with a vengeance to promote 'Freaky Styley'. The critical acclaim began to stack up in Lindy Goetz' management offices. "'Freaky Styley' is the first record of the rest of your life," wrote Glenn O'Brien in People magazine. Rolling Stone's Ira Robbins took a wider look at the crossover phenomenon that the band had wholeheartedly embraced.

"Popular music is in the midst of an overdue and exciting effort to integrate itself. The Red Hot Chili Peppers' quasi-orthodox hard funk might appear to be an imitation of 'black' music for a white audience, the band are actually irreverent, punky rockers with a jones of rhythm and blues vernacular and a commitment to humour, variety and unbridled stylistic independence."

The fact that four white men could play hardcore party funk seemed to amaze only that particular bible of hippy '60s ideology. In 1986, the groundswell was about to avalanche over all these dumb preconceptions. Rick Rubin's Raising Hell tour was a runaway smash hit, featuring Run DMC, the Beastie Boys and LL Cool J.

The band toured from October 1985 until March 1986. It was a riot of well-attended shows and limitless opportunities to sample – as Anthony Kiedis called his conquests – "the local delicacies".

One such "delicacy" remembers the first of two shows at Seattle's Astor Park club. "None of the band had that big rock star attitude which a lot of others carry around," she says. "One of my friends told me about the socks thing. It sounded like it could be fun.

"You met them like you'd meet any young, horny, good-looking guy, and whether they were about to go on stage or had just come off, they were just the same."

The girl is sure that the voice begging Anthony to fuck her during 'Party On Your Pussy' (retitled 'Special Secret Song' and recorded for their third album the following year) was hers.

"I knew the hotel they were staying at," she laughs. "And I probably got carried away a bit. But there again, so did he."

With typical grace, Kiedis will only say: "My brain was in a state of cosmic blossom!"

The band's lust would not always be so enthusiastically sated. One established rock magazine banned the Red Hot Chili Peppers from its pages when a relative of the publisher claimed she had been sexually harassed backstage!

The tour wound its way through the West Coast underground circuit, attracting full-on Frat Party numbskulls and precocious damsels. The Red Hot Chili Peppers were still a selective attraction, but the word was constantly spreading. In San Diego they were supported by a baby invention soon to be known as Guns N'Roses, and featuring another ex-Fairfax graduate, Slash.

Most came to see the Chili Peppers destroy a few boundaries and whip up a maelstrom of funked-up frenzy. They also came in the hope of catching a glimpse of the now-infamous socks-on-cocks routine.

"It's when you take a loud microphone in front of thousands of people," Flea told Sky magazine, "and you pull out your big Hollywood dick and you smack it against the mic in a percussive way, synchronising with the cock-smacking of the other three fellas, to form one big cock orchestra!"

It was also the last tour with drummer Cliff Martinez. Although originally hired for recording duties on 'The Red Hot Chili Peppers' debut, Martinez had remained behind the Pepper kit for longer than anyone had anticipated. It was simply time for Martinez to move on.

Jack Irons remembers getting a phone call out of the blue.

"It was Flea. He just said 'do you want to rejoin the Peppers?' I didn't say anything. It was something I had to think about very seriously, so I left it on hold for a little while. But finally I decided to do it."

What Is This? had continued to grow and flourish behind the Red Hot Chili Peppers. They had scored a minor hit with a cover of The Spinners' 'I'll Be Around' and were currently preparing work for their second MCA album. "I could feel that my part in the band was lessening," Irons remembers. "I never really liked the direction in which we were moving; things had changed."

Accepting Flea's offer to re-join the Red Hot Chili Peppers for the first time since lending a helping hand at the Rhythm Lounge all those jokes ago, Jack Irons completed the Los Faces reunion. What Is This? would only continue for a matter of months before simply grinding to a halt.

Jack Irons was the only Red Hot Chili Pepper actively to stay clear of drugs. "I was so against the whole thing that nobody ever wanted to hear my shit," he said.

RED HOT CHILI PEPPERS
SUGAR AND SPICE

Flea admitted using minor narcotics purely for recreational and creative purposes. Hillel Slovak and Anthony Kiedis, meanwhile, had spun out of control. It has been noted that Flea actually recruited Jack Irons in order to have an ally in the fight to save the band from auto-destruction. Because the Red Hot Chili Peppers were literally falling apart.

Every pimp, pusher and crazoid psycho supplier in every town would lie in wait for the Red Hot Chili Peppers as they set out on tour that autumn. It was not just the musical reputation which preceded them. The Red Hot Chili Peppers were now known users.

Hillel and Anthony's heroin addiction was ripping the heart out of the band. Backstage, fierce arguments would rage as Flea and Jack Irons desperately tried to hammer some sort of sense out of the guitarist and showman.

Sometimes these arguments would collapse into fights. Sometimes the band would play as a three-piece when Hillel failed to make it back to the venue in time, or when he was unconscious and unable to move. Sometimes the whole show was simply cancelled due to 'illness'.

"It's when you take a loud microphone in front of thousands of people and you pull out your big Hollywood dick and you smack it against the mic in a percussive way, synchronising with the cock-smacking of the other three fellas, to form one big cock orchestra!"

"It was one of those 'whore tours'," Anthony recalls. "We didn't have a new record out. We wanna rock the nation and make money at the same time. Touring is like a time warp. It's mostly hotels and soundchecks, but we have some fun. You travel and meet people and play music. You see and experience all kinds of nutty, wild-ass experiences."

Heroin killed the boredom. It was also killing the band.

59

"The whole process was grinding to a halt," says Jack Irons.
Alain Johannes remembers the desperate situation. "Jack could only do so much to stop the rot. He was the only solid centre in the group, the one who would pull everything together and make sure the next gig ever happened at all. He had his hands full just keeping Hillel on track. Jack kept Hillel alive for years."

Not only was the band's personal environment deteriorating, but so also was the relationship with EMI. Neither album had made a particularly large dent anywhere in the world, although both 'The Red Hot Chili Peppers' and 'Freaky Styley' had each cleared approximately 75,000 units. But America is a huge country, and such figures did not look too healthy on the EMI balance sheets.

At the same time, the Raising Hell tour had proved that white metal-funk-rap music was indeed the bright new thing. Although the Chili Peppers were playing to an average of 1,000 people a night and securing rave reviews from the alternative and underground media, mainstream success still seemed to be frustratingly elusive. American radio was wary of the band's reputation and remained stoutly unconvinced.

EMI in Los Angeles decided to opt out of the Chili Peppers' strategy and pass all control over to their East Coast operations. EMI (Manhattan), the LA boardroom figured, had hands-on experience at marketing such an awkward mutant as the Red Hot Chili Peppers.

Meanwhile, Flea had distanced himself from the emotionally shredded shell of the band. Frustrated by Anthony and Hillel's apathy, he dived into a succession of solo opportunities that could at least distract his thoughts from the awful possibility that the Red Hot Chili Peppers might not last the year.

He teamed up with ex-P.i.L guitarist Keith Levine and recorded two songs ('I'm Looking For Something' and 'Tang! Ting') for the 'Violent Opposition' EP. Flea also convinced Levine to use Hillel Slovak on a song called 'If Six Was Nine' on the same EP. Ironically, Hillel's performance on this one track is still regarded by many as the guitarist's finest minutes.

The bassist landed small parts in two movies – Iguana and Stranded, and finally proposed to his girlfriend Loesha. He had her name tattooed around his left nipple. Loesha was eight years Flea's junior and just out of High School. The marriage would not last.

But the most spectacular thing Flea did was to tell a sympathetic Press that Anthony Kiedis had enrolled on a course of drug rehabilitation. Kiedis had done no such thing, but Flea told the story anyway in the hope that it might just jolt his friend out of the wreckage of addiction. It would not be the last time that Flea would have to resort to such brutal tactics.

REDHOTCHILI PEPPERS
SUGAR AND SPICE

Kiedis was forced to admit through gritted teeth: "I'd found drugs had stopped being a good time, and they were consuming too much of my time and becoming a negative influence instead of a mind-opening one."

The Red Hot Chili Peppers, and particularly Anthony Kiedis, were about to embark on a course of self-discovery. This private exorcism would prove to be the foundation stone of the band's third studio album for their new masters in Manhattan.

It was also the last record they would make with Hillel Slovak.

The Red Hot Chili Peppers were not ready to make another record. The gruelling 'Whore Tour' had taken its toll and, with two full-blown addicts in the ranks, the band needed time and space to sort out their differences.

EMI (Manhattan) were not about to offer a respite. As far as they could see, the Red Hot Chili Peppers were in the right place (America) at the right time (a quarter past Rick Rubin) to capitalise on the new rap metal boom. They needed an album. Already the likes of Firehose, Fishbone and Faith No More were beginning to snap at the heels of the upstart crossover masters. The Red Hot Chili Peppers, wading through the thick soup of internal bickering, hadn't written enough material. Nonetheless, the record label began to search for a strict new taskmaster to produce the band.

Rick Rubin walked out of a scheduled meeting with the Red Hot Chili Peppers after barely one hour.

"It was a very unhealthy feeling in the room," he later said. "Just bad news, negativity all around, lack of organisation between the members and a lack of trust. Really not a good feeling."

This was typical of the band at the time. Flea and Jack Irons would protect their own sober corner. Anthony and Hillel would be all over the place. Neither limb seemed to know what the other was doing. Worse, neither seemed to care particularly.

Salvation came in the form of bad medicine. Michael Beinhorn was under strict instructions to sort out the Red Hot Chili Peppers. Flea admits that Beinhorn was certainly the "coolest" producer they interviewed. When Beinhorn – who had risen rapidly up the producers' ladder with his work for such beige funk acts as Herbie Hancock and Nona Hendryx – discovered that the Chili Peppers had only sketched out the grand total of five songs for the album, he was furious.

Where others had coddled (George Clinton) and endured (Andy Gill), Beinhorn would shout and confront. It was a short, sharp shock and one that undoubtedly inspired the band. Beinhorn knew about the Chili Peppers' problems. His decision to bustle them into a collective activity began to reap rewards.

RED HOT CHILI PEPPERS
SUGAR AND SPICE

Beinhorn wisely refused to allow the band anywhere near a costly recording studio until, at the very least, the five songs had been hammered out into workable shapes. The producer became an unofficial secretary; working hard to organise the band and arrange every aspect of the pre-production process.

Only when he considered the band to be able to deliver the album they all imagined, did Beinhorn book the Red Hot Chili Peppers into Los Angeles' Capitol Studios. It was now May 1987. It was here that 'The Uplift Mofo Party Plan' was enlarged, polished and finally executed with a nuclear mixture of adrenalin and testosterone.

As Anthony Kiedis would later explain to one of the first European journalists to interview the band (Kerrang!'s Paul Henderson): "It's (the record) got the energy of a million stampeding elephants, the ferocity of a million hawks diving for little green mice in the fields... and the diversity of a pigeon's feather."

The Uplift Mofo Party Plan' was a big record. It sounded huge. It had funk and metal and Rage and Beauty and Sex and Style... and parental advisory stickers. It would not be the last rock album to fall foul of the PMRC – the ratchet-faced collection of Washington wives who have as much political clout as they have a bad case of moral paranoia. At the time the group (formed in 1985) was a worrying development. Record companies marketing albums deemed to be 'unsavoury' by a panel of self-confessed "golden-oldies" (Pam Howar, Susan Baker and Elizabeth Gore) would be subjected to a barrage of official complaints from the PMRC via the RIAA (the Recording Industry Association of America). This could include anything from Madonna to Cyndi Lauper, Judas Priest to 2 Live Crew.

'The Uplift Mofo Party Plan' came under attack for 'Party On Your Pussy'. It was consequently stickered by EMI (Manhattan), an act which would considerably narrow the chances of all-important radio play.

The song was typical Red Hot Chili Peppers: a clatter of nutty funk and sexually explicit primal energy. It wasn't the greatest song on 'The Uplift Mofo Party Plan', but it soon became one of the most notorious in the band's repertoire. The song was actually hidden from the passing punter's psyche. 'Party On Your Pussy' was advertised on the album's track listing as 'Special Secret Song Inside'.

Despite the repeated charges of misogyny directed at Anthony Kiedis by numerous sections of the media (but, ironically, never by the fans who bought the records), 'The Uplift Mofo Party Plan' was widely regarded as a far deeper and more soul-searching affair.

In particular, 'Fight Like A Brave' (the first single to be lifted from the album) was written by Kiedis about his and Hillel's growing heroin isolation.

63

"It's a song," he later explained, "which tries to encourage someone who feels as though they're grovelling in the gutter of life. It's an encouragement to tell them that no matter how low you've gone, there's always hope for a revival, whether it's spiritual or mental."

Similarly, the eco-friendly 'Behind The Sun' was overlooked as a single by EMI for almost five years! This, despite the band's own conviction that the song was the most radio-friendly on the album. They would later to be proved entirely correct.

The Red Hot Chili Peppers' cover of Bob Dylan's 20-year-old 'Subterranean Homesick Blues' was suggested by fellow friends and musicians in Thelonius Monster. It became apparent that it was certainly not Kiedis' idea when he explained, in rather less colourful language than usual, that: "Funk comes in all shapes and sizes. I'm sure there is some brand of funk to be deciphered in Bob Dylan's music!"

> *"It's got the energy of a million stampeding elephants, the ferocity of a million hawks diving for little green mice in the fields... and the diversity of a pigeon's feather."*

The band also covered Hendrix's 'Fire', although it never made it onto 'The Uplift Mofo Party Plan' itself. Instead it later cropped up on the band's 'Abbey Road' EP alongside three more takes from the album sessions.

'The Organic Anti-Beat Box Band' was a self-depreciating comment on not only Flea's purist mistrust of drum machines, but also maybe on their experiences recording the first album with Andy Gill.

"I used to be totally anti-drum machine," the bassist said. "Now I'm amazed by the artistic creativity of someone like Hank Shocklee. He makes these amazing collages of sound that have so much emotional value."

The fuss stirred up by 'Special Secret Song Inside' began to overshadow the album's nitro-virtuosity. It would keep returning to haunt them for a good few years. To this day, Kiedis is weary of having to explain the song away and to justify his position.

"People get the impression that we did something they choose to read as being sexist," he told The Face's Mandi James. "I really don't feel consciously sexist, though maybe growing up in this environment I can't help having some inbred attitudes. But I certainly don't regard women as being any less capable than men.

"Look, I'm sexually attracted to women. I don't have a fear of voicing that in the music that we make. But I don't look at them as just sex objects.

"I don't really care what people think. We got slammed for 'Party On Your Pussy'. But, y'know, I have not met any sexually-active heterosexual man who is not attracted to a woman's body and did not worship or respect it. We're just voicing carnal feelings which everybody experiences.

"What people want is a sensitive caring relationship with someone with whom you can share all sorts of beautiful things. But sometimes, don't you just wanna go out and get crazy and fuck like a wild banshee? People don't like talking about it but they all have those feelings. Suppressing them only causes sexual frustration, bitterness and unhappiness."

Flea: "Y'know, Anthony writes so many lyrics that are obviously straight from the heart ('Fight Like A Brave'), but no-one's bothered to look at them before. The Red Hot Chili Peppers are about a love for everybody; we're not misogynous, we're not homophobic, we're not racist. We care about humanity."

It was a particular creed that would be severely tested over the coming months, as once again the Red Hot Chili Peppers set out on the road to support the release of 'The Uplift Mofo Party Plan'. It was a long tour with no particular ending in sight. For Hillel Slovak, it was a daunting prospect.

For the time being, however, Flea was quite happy to talk to People magazine about the band's "secret plan".

"First step was to make a great record. Second step was to make a great video. And the third step was to make a great tour. We figure we've done step one with 'The Uplift Mofo Party Plan'. As far as that record goes, I think it's the most complete record we've ever made, in that I'm happy with every aspect of it. I think it's captured the live intensity of the band, and it's captured different aspects of what we do musically."

The Red Hot Chili Peppers' tour kicked off in the autumn of 1987 with Faith No More supporting. At the time, the two bands harboured no animosity towards each other since the billing seemed to reflect accurately both bands' status.

Faith No More were obviously inspired by the Peppers, yet they could boast spacey keyboards and the man-monolith guitarist, Big Jim Martin, to keep a separate identity intact. Faith No More still had a long way to go before they smashed through the underground rut with 'The Real Thing'.

When Faith No More eventually burst out the MTV traps with their 'Epic' single, the Red Hot Chili Peppers in general, and Anthony Kiedis in particular, were not amused. They had laboured through endless years of obscurity, only for Faith No More to steal most of their funk metal thunder. By this time Faith No More had sacked their original vocalist, Chuck Moseley, and replaced him with Mike Patton just prior to the band's international breakthrough. It was widely noted that Patton had obviously been studying Kiedis' own stage mannerisms for some years. In Europe, especially, Faith No More had a head start over the Red Hot Chili Peppers in terms of popularity.

"It really bothered me," Kiedis confessed years later. "I thought, 'what a drag if people get the idea that I'm actually ripping him (Patton) off!

"After it stewed in my stomach for a while, I just decided to accept it. He's just a kid. Besides, without his left foot he's going to have to change. We planned to kidnap Patton, shave off his hair and saw off one of his feet. Just so he'd be forced to find a style of his own!"

For the time being, however, the two bands were happy to tour together in a frenetic funk metal package. It swept across the country from one 700-capacity venue to another, occasionally breaking through into larger auditoriums in New York and Atlanta, but only to return to the smaller clubs the following night.

"The strain manifests itself in different ways," Flea explained to Rocky Mountain News reporter Justin Mitchell. "Mainly with us being sick of each other, little things that get on our nerves being magnified about fifty billion times. It's like being stuck in the same mobile home with eight other people for days at a time. You wind up sticking the gerbil in the fish tank!"

The most noticeable victim of this combat stress was Hillel Slovak. Since the 'Whore Tour' he had regressed deeper into his own private heroin hole. Some nights he would blankly play one song for the entire set, immune to his fellow band-members prompting and pleas. Other nights he would be playing so loud that the sound crew would have to turn him down from the front-of-house desk. Some nights they would simply turn Hillel off completely. The guitarist never even noticed.

It was a situation that was rapidly heading towards a showdown. In early 1988, Hillel's state was affecting not only the Red Hot Chili Peppers' performances but also the entire atmosphere of the tour. Flea, Anthony and Jack would talk behind Hillel's back. They would talk long into the night trying to find the solution.

67

68

RED HOT CHILI PEPPERS
SUGAR AND SPICE

Eventually they decided to remove the problem altogether and sack their close friend from the band. Anthony Kiedis decided to tell Hillel after a show at the Bayou club in Washington DC at the end of April.

The Red Hot Chili Peppers never told Hillel Slovak that he was no longer needed. It was something that Fishbone's Angelo Moore said to Anthony as he sat trying to think of how to break the news to Hillel. Fishbone had replaced Faith No More as tour support over Christmas.

"Don't do it, man," was all the sax player said. Anthony knew immediately what Angelo was saying, and he was stunned.

"Mainly with us being sick of each other, little things that get on our nerves being magnified about fifty billion times. It's like being stuck in the same mobile home with eight other people for days at a time. You wind up sticking the gerbil in the fish tank!"

"It had a really profound effect on me. It dawned on me that we did, in fact, have to stick together if we wanted to stay alive. Hillel didn't need us. We needed Hillel.

"The term 'drug addict' doesn't mean that you're a bad guy, it means you've got a problem, a sickness. It's a disease that can afflict anybody, just like heart disease."

Flea remembers one of the last things he and Hillel ever agreed upon. Flea's wife was expecting a baby. He was a long way from her side and he would constantly telephone for an up-date on the pregnancy. Hillel was convinced that Loesha would give birth to a baby girl. He would be proved right. Loesha gave birth to baby Clara just days after Hillel's death. Today Flea admits that Clara is the one thing that reminds him of Hillel Slovak more than anything else in the world.

"At the time it was real hard for me to tell him to his face how much I loved him," Anthony later admitted. "I wanted to tell him that we had the Red Hot Chili Peppers in common, we had our friendship in common, we grew up together, we loved each other. I wanted to tell him that I wanted to spend my life making music with him."

Instead of telling Hillel how he felt to his face, Anthony Kiedis wrote the guitarist a series of letters and notes. No-one really knew just how deep Hillel had fallen. Instead, says Anthony, Flea and Jack Irons were sometimes more concerned about the Chili Peppers' frontman himself.

"They were all afraid that I was going to die because I would just take too much too often for too long a period of time.

"Hillel was much more subtle and much more cunning in his disguise. He had everyone believing that he had it under control."

Instead of sacking Hillel, the Red Hot Chili Peppers made a concerted effort to nurse their guitarist through his 'sickness'. The 'Uplift Mofo Party Plan' had surpassed both the band's and EMI's expectations by levelling off at Number 143 in the Billboard charts. It was nowhere compared to the likes of Gloria Estefan, Foreigner, and Terence Trent D'Arby, but it proved that the Red Hot Chili Peppers could indeed make a commercial record.

They were about to embark on their first European tour and it was a territory that was important to the band. To return from Europe with critical acclaim would be a feather in their cap. Hillel and Anthony agreed to stop using heroin for the entire duration of the tour. They just could not afford to fuck up in Europe. They would need to be clean in order to re-establish the band all over again. Europe knew little of the Red Hot Chili Peppers. The Red Hot Chili Peppers knew less about Europe.

1988 was a good year for the Red Hot Chili Peppers to hit the United States of Europe. The booming yuppy culture had turned pop music into a designer accessory alongside the mobile phone, the Filofax and the Porsche 911. It was a vacuum out there. It was a time for feelgood pop fodder such as Bros, Kylie and INXS.

Conversely, it was a celebrity charity year. The Prince Of Wales' Prince's Trust gala concert featured Wet Wet Wet and Rick Astley. Bryan Adams and George Michael inexplicably celebrated Nelson Mandela's 70th birthday at Wembley Stadium. The enormous Live Aid extravaganza had opened everybody's eyes to the possibility of the Super-Charity Event. Rock stars were playing God, dressing in their shiny suits like so many rockin' bishops and saints.

71

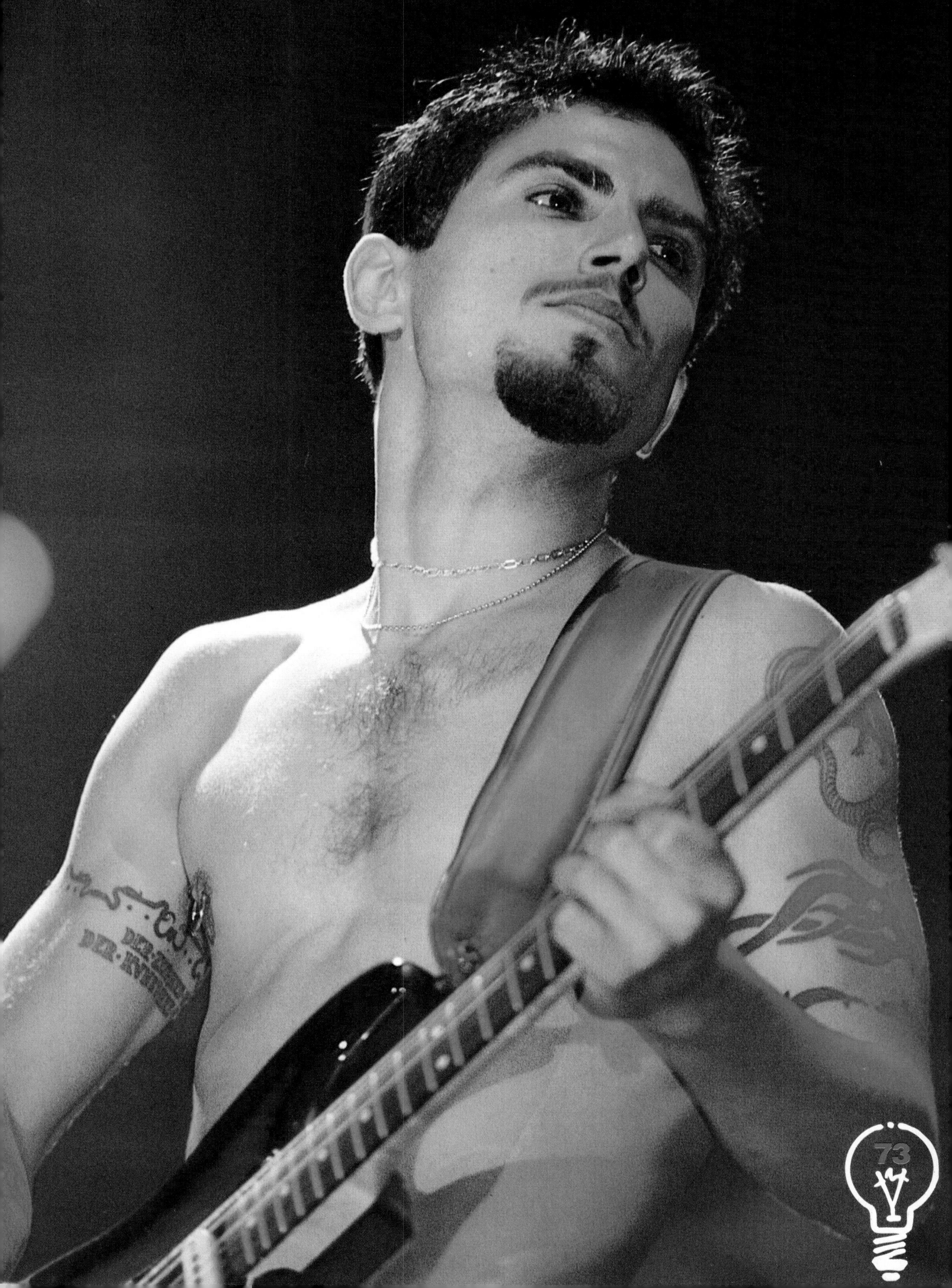

It was the Grab Culture epitomised by comedian Harry Enfield's alter-ego, Loadsamoney. The self-employed builder crashed straight into the Top Five with his boorish anthem of greed and consumption. Harry Enfield would later abandon Loadsamoney when it became more than apparent that the people who found him the funniest were those same people Enfield was trying to vilify.

These were conservative times. These were people that needed a kick up the motor systems like never before. Anthony Kiedis waved that week's music press around his head as the red-eye flight began its approach into Heathrow. He offered the papers to Flea and asked if the bassist wanted to read about the competition.

"Well you can't!" Kiedis bellowed, snatching back the paper. "Because there isn't any!"

The world of British hard rock had turned American. Save for the likes of Def Leppard and Iron Maiden, the old school of heavy metal had pretty much imploded. The likes of Wolfsbane and the Quireboys were being discussed as the next wave of global gladiators. Neither would ever achieve much outside of the UK.

The rock charts were dominated by the likes of Van Halen's 'OU 812', Poison's 'Open Up & Say Ahh!' and Bon Jovi's 'Slippery When Wet'. Out in the pubs and clubs of London, baby Zodiac Mindwarps and lumpen Metallica wannabes cluttered up the circuit.

But the rock media in Britain would be the first to welcome the Red Hot Chili Peppers with open arms, even if the writers didn't necessarily know quite what to make of the band's riot of colour. Living Colour and Kings X had, in some minor way, introduced funk metal to the UK. Yet these two eminently sensible acts simply could not compete with the Chili Peppers' primal performance.

The Red Hot Chili Peppers' principal task was to establish a fan-base in the UK. The infinitely smaller British arm of the EMI corporation had turned down the chance to release the band's albums. They could not understand quite where the music would fit into their domestic musical climate. Rather than take a gamble on 'The Red Hot Chili Peppers', 'Freaky Styley' and 'The Uplift Mofo Party Plan' being an alternative to the blank mainstream, EMI (UK) had released just one single ('Hollywood') to test the waters. It was afforded little promotion and the Red Hot Chili Peppers had consequently been relegated to the label's backburner.

Reports of the band's activities, especially the socks-on-cocks routine, had reached the London media via the magazines' American stringers in California. Yet no-one really knew what the band would offer. The Red Hot Chili Peppers would have to start over again to prove themselves.

74

REDHOTCHILIPEPPERS
SUGARANDSPICE

Flea, Anthony, Hillel and Jack were not overtly worried about this particular scenario. If there was one thing the Red Hot Chili Peppers could guarantee, it was a live show to rival any of their peers. They hit London running.

They based themselves in the Columbia Hotel – the notorious London hotel whose distinctly vague licensing laws made it a favourite with rock bands on every level. Anthony, Flea, and Jack greeted the succession of interested foreigners like gentlemen. They would patiently explain the Red Hot Chili Peppers' manifesto whilst Hillel Slovak quietly suffered minor withdrawal symptoms in his room upstairs. Hillel seldom made it down for photographs. Hillel did, however, make it to Abbey Road studios for the now infamous photograph which graced the jacket of their 'Abbey Road' EP. The four Chili Peppers were snapped striding across the famous zebra crossing wearing nothing except their well-stuffed socks. The photograph was taken at 6am, before the city had awoken and before the usual coachloads of tourists and descended on Abbey Road to pay homage to the Fab Four. It was circulated to the British press, but only really served to highlight the band's reputation as a zany oddity.

"Europe was crazy," Jack Irons recalls. "The sock thing had got completely out of hand; it was really demanding. The Red Hot Chili Peppers were doing things that a lot of people thought were funny and were jokes. But whenever we played the songs we were very serious about playing. It was just the presentation which seemed goofy or loony. It was actually a very serious goofiness. There was a method to the madness."

EMI (UK) released the 'Abbey Road' EP on May 16. It featured 'Backwoods', 'Hollywood', 'True Men Don't Kill Coyotes', 'Catholic School Girls Rule', and the cover of Hendrix's 'Fire' which had been recorded but never used on 'The Uplift Mofo Party Plan'. As a taster for the live shows ahead it fulfilled its purpose, but little else. The band were already on the road in Europe with the Ramones.

The three British shows, however, gave the press and public alike the opportunity to savour the sensory explosion which the band could invoke. "The sound kills at 50 paces," wrote Kerrang!'s Phil Wilding, describing the magic inside Camden's Electric Ballroom. "It throws punters off the stage and rises as an awesome cloud that destroys preconceived ideas – musically or otherwise – without the merest bat of an eyelid."

To the Red Hot Chili Peppers, however, it was like turning the clock back three years. They had already stamped their authority as a live act across America's West Coast. Their reputation for fun and mayhem meant that they were now a fairly safe bet for any promoter in the States. Their third album for a major label had established the band as a commercially viable entity. Yet here they were having to talk about socks again. No-one wanted to talk to the band about the music or the message. They had specifically recorded 'Fire' to re-establish the band's musical approach under the weight of a media more interested in the

75

REDHOTCHILIPEPPERS
SUGARANDSPICE

tales of sex and drugs. The band had never made it easy for their music to be taken seriously. Indeed, they had only formed for a one-off joke way back at the Rhythm Lounge. But now they felt that the (sometimes grudging) credit they were being afforded back home was deserved. Flea and Anthony Kiedis had persevered with this thing that they both loved as much as they loved life itself.

Although the live shows were almost unanimously successful, Europe had yet to appreciate the accomplished musical backbone which held the performance together. It would, everyone agreed, take time.

The Red Hot Chili Peppers were exhausted when they returned to Los Angeles in the middle of June. They needed a week or so to recover from the European jaunt. They needed time to sit and think and dream and just take a deep breath. EMI were already discussing the next album. The whole band felt that these plans could wait for just a couple of weeks.

Flea, Anthony, Jack and Hillel didn't talk much for a week. Flea's wife was about to give to birth to baby Clara. Jack was thinking of maybe contacting Alain Johannes to see how his friend's recording project was taking shape.

It was no secret on the streets that both Anthony and Hillel were back on heroin. They had promised each other that they would stay clean for Europe and see how long sobriety would last once they touched back down at LA International airport. Jack and Flea were disgusted to hear that it had only lasted a few hours. Both retreated back to the sanctuary of the warm domestic nest.

And then Hillel Slovak was dead.

Hillel Slovak died on June 27, 1988. He was 26 years old. He died alone in his apartment on a Saturday night. His body was not discovered until Monday morning when a friend happened to call.

An autopsy was performed on that Monday afternoon by the Los Angeles' district coroner. A representative issued a statement to the Press saying that the circumstances surrounding Hillel's death were "inconclusive". This is usual Establishment-speak to protect the immediate family's feelings.

According to Jewish custom, the dead must be laid to rest as soon as possible. Hillel Slovak was buried at 1pm on Tuesday, June 30, in Mount Sinai Memorial Park. A small obituary ran in the LA Times that morning.

And that was it. Hillel Slovak – guitarist in the Red Hot Chili Peppers – was history.

79

RED**HOT**CHILI**PEPPERS**
SUGARAND**SPICE**

Chapter 8

Nothing happened for a while. There was an awful period of disbelief. And then the Red Hot Chili Peppers collapsed with grief. The fact that the band had lost a guitarist was utterly and completely irrelevant to Flea, Anthony and Jack. It didn't matter. There were a million guitarists in Los Angeles. For now, and for several weeks to follow Hillel's death, the band itself simply did not exist in anyone's thoughts.

Hillel's death had torn apart the four Los Faces from High School. They had lost a friend, a brother, a conspirator, a lover, an artist, a soulmate and a spirit. But the remaining Los Faces felt so fucking helpless. Their friend had died alone. He had slipped through the white light unconscious and unnoticed. He had been a phone call away, and yet they had done nothing to check up on Hillel.

Guilt confused their grief. It would be a long time before Anthony, Flea and Jack would recover emotionally from the knowledge that they might have been able to save Hillel.

It took Anthony over a year to admit: "I could have saved him. I know CPR really well, and I've brought back a couple of friends who died from an OD."

Hillel Slovak did not die a hero. Compared to the deaths of Freddie Mercury, Janis Joplin, John Lennon, Kurt Cobain, and the ever-growing list of celebrity casualties, Hillel's was not a big rock'n'roll death. The fact that Hillel died of an overdose before realising even half the Chili Peppers' potential makes it all the more senseless. It was an ordinary death. It was a squalid death. But the most damaging aspect as far as the Red Hot Chili Peppers were concerned was that Hillel's was a totally unexpected death.

"I knew he was doing drugs," Flea would later explain, "but I didn't expect him to die. It's like one minute he's standing next to me on stage joking and playing, and the next minute he's dead."

As a fellow addict, Anthony Kiedis was crushed and devastated by his friend's overdose. It could, Kiedis immediately realised, so easily have been him. He found this impossible to deal with.

Anthony Kiedis walked out of the memorial service, grabbed a few essentials from his apartment and drove down into Mexico. He just drove in a daze. For a month he lived on the beach. He made his life as simple as possible whilst he came to terms with Hillel's death. He was self-sufficient but, more importantly, he was clean. He was determined to stay clean.

Anthony Kiedis would not touch another drug again in his life.

Jack Irons, who had known Hillel in his pre-teens and who had grown up in the same Jewish neighbourhood, simply could not cope. He remembered their early Kiss routines, their joint struggle to master their respective instruments, and their gradual rise through the Fairfax hierarchy with Alain Johannes in Anthym.

All of this haunted Jack until, fearing for his safety, his family committed him to psychiatric care. He didn't protest at their decision, he just withdrew. His drums were boxed up and kept in storage. Jack stopped caring about anything except Hillel Slovak.

"All of a sudden," he would later say, "all my feelings had been taken away from me."

Jack Irons would not remain in care for long. It would, however, take an offer from Joe Strummer to coax him back behind his drum kit. Jack Irons would never play drums again for the Red Hot Chili Peppers.

It was Flea who put on the bravest facade. He threw himself into Loesha's happiness and mourned in private. He watched the band suddenly disintegrate in a matter of days as Anthony disappeared and Jack began to drown.

Flea hated the fact that he had deliberately distanced himself from Hillel over the course of the past year and that he had done little to encourage or treat his friend. But no-one could have seen this disastrous outcome.

"Knowing I'll never have the chance to share anything with him again is the worst thing," the bassist commented at the time.

Flea was adamant that Hillel's death was not going to mark the death of the Red Hot Chili Peppers. Instead, Flea would somehow resurrect this thing and dedicate its success to Hillel Slovak. Right now, however, all Flea could do was cry.

"One of the weirdest things about him dying," Flea would tell Rolling Stone years later, "was that all the inside jokes we had between us, just from sitting around being silly, died with Hillel."

Until he burst back into his life on August 1, Flea toyed with the idea of re-grouping the Red Hot Chili Peppers without Anthony Kiedis. He and Lindy Goetz would discuss this scenario endlessly, even going so far as to audition a couple of likely replacements.

"Yeah, well," Anthony would later admit to The Face's Mandi James, "they fired me once. They tried to hire in some other geek and it just didn't fly."

These attempts, however, were only half-hearted. Flea never really intended to get rid of his close friend. The bassist just wanted to play music.

REDHOTCHILIPEPPERS
SUGARANDSPICE

And then Anthony Kiedis returned from Mexico. The two would constantly refer to this reunion in terms of a re-birth.

"Flea and I realised that the Red Hot Chili Peppers was life to us," Anthony said. "It was both an outlet and a lifeline. We needed to hold onto it.

"The death of Hillel changed our entire attitude. Losing your best friend at the age of 26 is a mind and soul-blower. But there was definitely an inspiration which came from Hillel dying, which helped sharpen the focus of the band. Flea and I were left with each other and we decided 'Here's something we started a long time ago and that we haven't finished'.

"One of the weirdest things about him dying, was that all the inside jokes we had between us, just from sitting around being silly, died with Hillel."

"We had to bear down, change our lifestyles and look at what was important to us – things like friendship, love, making great music and not getting sidetracked by the more negative influences in life. We tried to use our loss as a bolstering, positive influence – if nothing else, to prove to the world that what we were doing was worthy and legitimate. Hillel may be dead, but we're not."

Flea didn't expand much, beyond commenting: "Anthony has always been the man of fucking steel! The fact that he is as healthy as he is, and weathered the shit he has weathered, is amazing!"

It would take the Red Hot Chili Peppers a full year get back up to speed.

REDHOTCHILIPEPPERS
SUGARANDSPICE

84

Chapter 9

ohn Frusciante was a natural born Chili Pepper. One of the very first things he ever told the Press was that all he really cared about was "playing guitar like I've got a huge cock!".

Frusciante was only 18 when he introduced himself to Flea. He had seen the Red Hot Chili Peppers for the first time over 3 years ago at the Los Angeles Variety Arts Centre. From that moment on, he claimed, "their music meant everything to me".

Frusciante was a strange, shy individual who had never played in a band. Punk, to Frusciante, was "your war against those fucking average white, suburban, bland idiots who were destroying the world".

Alone in his bedroom, he would practise guitar for up to 15 hours a day. He would jam to Hendrix and Zappa, totally immersing himself in the music just as Hillel Slovak had done ten years before. In the evenings he would persuade everyone he knew to come and see the Chili Peppers. Sometimes he would even buy their tickets for them.

"I just thought that everybody should see the Red Hot Chili Peppers," he later said, "because I thought they were the most fantastic thing to hit the earth."

This fanaticism earned John Frusciante the chance to jam with Flea in the band's rehearsal studio. Flea was impressed, but did not seriously consider this space hero to be a likely contender, though he invited him back to his house to work through a few ideas on a 4-track machine. Flea was also impressed with Frusciante's input and attitude, but still unsure whether his lack of experience in a band would hinder the Chili Peppers' stage show. Frusciante, however, was a marked man in Flea's mind.

The Red Hot Chili Peppers had publicly resurfaced early in September 1988 for an appearance live on MTV's 120 Minutes alternative rock show. The line-up had been hastily assembled and rigorously rehearsed. Ex-George Clinton guitarist, Duane 'Blackbyrd' McKnight, and ex-Dead Kennedy's drummer Darren 'DH' Peligro, had been recruited for their masterful funk and punk legacies respectively.

"At this point," says Flea, "I'd say we were rawer and sloppier than before. We'd played together as a band for years, and it wasn't until now that I realised how tight we'd got."

This was a typically stoic comment from Flea. The reality of the situation was that neither McKnight nor Peligro could hold a light to Hillel and Jack Irons.

McKnight finally bowed out of the band after just four shows.

Flea remembered the few hours he had spent in the company of John Frusciante. He told Anthony Kiedis, but it would take a miracle to convince the pair that they should enlist this young stage virgin.

When Thelonius Monster's Bob Forrest phoned Anthony Kiedis to ask his friend if he knew of any suitable guitarists, Kiedis was quick to recommend Frusciante. The young, chain-smoking freak, however, was so nervous of auditioning that he asked Flea and Anthony to accompany him to Thelonius Monster's rehearsal space. The two Chili Peppers agreed and dutifully introduced Frusciante to Bob Forrest. Flea and Anthony hung around the studio to watch their friend go through his considerable paces.

Bob Forrest was stunned at Frusciante's playing. Although wary – just like Kiedis and Flea – of recruiting a player with absolutely no stage experience whatsoever, it was an obvious talent that begged to be explored. Bob Forrest told John Frusciante immediately that he was 'in'.

Anthony and Bob Forrest reconvened for five minutes. Frusciante was confused. And then Anthony Kiedis turned to this skinny, nervous prodigy and said: "In the Red Hot Chili Peppers, that is!"

The Red Hot Chili Peppers made their public debut with John Frusciante on the syndicated and horribly-titled 2HIP4TV show. It was apparent from the very first note that Frusciante had been born to fill Hillel Slovak's space.

"John was an absolute Hillel clone," remembers Alain Johannes, watching as ever on the sidelines.

"Not only did he play like him, he stood like him and moved like him as well." Frusciante took to his new-found fame like a buffalo to a puddle. There were reports around town that the latest Chili Pepper was running amok. It was a period of adjustment for a painfully shy teenager who now found himself in the spotlight.

"That was to be expected," said Flea. "When you're 18 years old and you want to get laid really bad, and all of a sudden you're in a band the girls all want to fuck, you're bound to go crazy!"

It would take months for the real John Frusciante to emerge. Anthony and Flea let him find his feet in his own good time. Deep at heart, John Frusciante was an exceptionally private person who would rather gaze for hours at a Van Gogh painting than endure the rigours of the media treadmill. It was typical of Frusciante when, two years later, he suddenly and inexplicably abandoned Anthony Kiedis on a promotional visit to London and flew back home to LA.

Before he left, however, he told Melody Maker's Neil Perry that: "Any artist is connecting themselves with spiritual feelings – or should be – whether they verbalise it or not. Music and all art forms are originally completely separate worlds from those of money and business and ambition. It's about totally separating yourself from those worlds. When I listen to Captain Beefheart or read (William) Burroughs, those worlds to me are so much more real than the one I see when I walk down Sunset Boulevard and I feel like strangling someone just to remind them we're fucking alive, you know?"

"John was an absolute Hillel clone, not only did he play like him, he stood like him and moved like him as well."

In contrast to Frusciante, Chad Smith was a genial metal behemoth from the Mid West. He arrived at the audition and said very little. Flea, Anthony and John were equal parts amused, horrified and amazed at him.

Anthony remembers today that "the studio was being stormed by a herd of psychedelic gorillas!"

Chad Smith didn't just play his drums. He smashed his fists into the cymbals, his eyes bugged and wired, and he was shouting at Flea at the top his voice. "He was yelling stuff like 'Come on! Fuck! Piss! Doom! Come on!'. We were like, what the fuck?!"

Chad Smith simply hit everything as hard as he possibly could and bulldozed right through the middle of the Chili Peppers' audition. There had been around 30 auditions for a new drummer before him, but none of them could compete with Chad Smith. He was the only possible candidate to fill the aching gap left by Jack Irons.

Chad had arrived in Los Angeles from Detroit where he had played in a succession of local hard rock acts, most notably Toby Redd. They had been signed to Epic Records but had disbanded earlier that year. So Chad flung a few possessions into his beloved pick-up and drove out to LA to attend the Musicians Institute. It was here that he learnt of the Chili Peppers' search for a drummer to replace Duane Peligro, who had departed perfectly amicably a few days before.

"I just went in and rocked out!" Chad modestly recalls.

In March 1985, the Red Hot Chili Peppers delayed their plans to start work on their fourth album, and instead went out on the road to test the strength of this new machine. It was only a short tour of Florida, but it proved beyond a doubt that this massive tangled muscle was once again complete.

Not only were the Red Hot Chili Peppers complete, they were also as dry as a desert.

"Let's face it," said Flea, "anyone coming to see us, unless they're really thick-headed and stupid, would have the sense not to offer drugs around. That's a really unpopular thing around the Red Hot Chili Peppers."

John Frusciante enjoyed the attention as much as anyone. He left his mark on two female fans who approached him backstage to ask for his autograph. John Frusciante took their pen and paper and scrawled his intent:
"I want to destroy your hymens. Love John."

Michael Beinhorn had waited patiently for the Red Hot Chili Peppers to grieve, regroup and return to work. The producer had watched them on stage and in rehearsals, and he was adamant that they were ready to record their fourth album. He was also adamant that it would be the record finally to push the Chili Peppers over the edge of underground notoriety and into the mainstream. It was not, however, going to be a mainstream album. It was going to be a record for Everyman.

In a typically lurid frame of mind, Anthony Kiedis would later refer to each Chili Peppers' record in terms of the sexual act.

"We came out with the first record and we were kissing the world, caressing the neck and the ears. With the second record, we were taking off the shirt and fondling the breasts of the world. The third record, we got down to the panties. By the time we came to this album, things were getting very hard and soft and wet. It was about to happen."

For the time being, however, locked away inside Los Angeles' Ocean Sound studios, the Red Hot Chili Peppers were being soundly whipped by Michael Beinhorn.

Aware that his four lovable charges had a tendency to slack off if given half a chance, Beinhorn had instigated a strict regime that was implemented with unforgiving army efficiency. It was also a regime designed to prevent Anthony and Flea from slipping back into any negative, unproductive pit of self-pity. The Red Hot Chili Peppers were there to cut a record. They were not allowed to bring any ghosts into the studio with them.

Beinhorn told each member of the band: "Don't think you're in here simply to make a record. You're in here to fight a war."

Before they had left the pre-production studios, the producer had assembled the group in a tight circle around him. Just like a football manager's pep talk, he had fired the band up by screaming in their faces: "This is gonna be the greatest record ever made! This is gonna be the greatest record ever made!..."
The Red Hot Chili Peppers screamed back at their producer. It could not have been a more positive beginning.

The sessions, however, were fraught with tension. Flea and Anthony were used to Beinhorn's tough standards and at first were able to appreciate his uncompromising attitude. Chad Smith was more than willing to be bullied into delivering the performance of a lifetime. But John Frusciante hated it.

"We came out with the first record and we were kissing the world, caressing the neck and the ears. With the second record, we were taking off the shirt and fondling the breasts of the world. The third record, we got down to the panties. By the time we came to this album, things were getting very hard and soft and wet. It was about to happen."

The guitarist and the producer were at each other's throats from day one. Both were perfectionists and knew exactly what they were after. The problem was that they seemed to be after two totally different things. When one was satisfied the other insisted on just one more take, and vice versa.

Eventually the situation became unbearable. It was starting to affect Anthony and Flea. They were just not ready for such a bullish and brutal environment. When the sessions were deemed to have become unworkable by all parties concerned, the Red Hot Chili Peppers' fourth record consisted of just 38 minutes of music. The band relayed the news to EMI via Lindy Goetz. For a while it was an unhappy deadlock.

89

REDHOTCHILIPEPPERS
SUGARANDSPICE

REDHOTCHILIPEPPERS
SUGARANDSPICE

The record label dispatched an ambassador to the West Coast in order to judge the situation. It was indeed a mess. But the 38 minutes of recorded music were perhaps the most vivid and exhilarating moments anyone had heard from the band. More importantly, for the first time EMI heard hit singles. The company decided to go with what they had.

It was mutually agreed that the album would be brought up to full length by adding the band's cover of 'Fire' (originally recorded for 'The Uplift Mofo Party Plan' but only released on the 'Abbey Road' EP), and 'Taste The Pain' (a track recorded with Fishbone's drummer Fish for the 'Say Anything' movie soundtrack).

The Red Hot Chili Peppers decided to launch their new baby via a series of low-key live shows. The album was to be called 'Rocking Freakapotomus', but by the time they played the LA Hollywood Palace in July, a new title had replaced Anthony Kiedis' original aberration.

"Mother's milk," Anthony explained, "is a life-giving, nurturing, intoxicating, good-natured, health-building, loving, comforting, warm, soothing substance. When you drink it, it makes you feel good and makes you grow up strong and healthy. It wards off infection and disease. And it's honest. It's pure and wholesome, and that's what we like to think our music represents."

'Mother's Milk' was officially launched in early August 1989, at the New York New Music seminar. A select elite of music industry insiders were first directed to the glitzy Tramps nightclub, only to find that they were then instructed to cross the street to the city's only indoor miniature golf course! It amused the band.

Even the most jaded brain and heart was swept along by this gleeful assault of Pepperdom. 'Mother's Milk' was the first album of the rest of the Chili Peppers' life.

The record was all things to every reviewer. To Playboy it was "the most dynamic punk funk connection you're likely to hear for a long time." To the Washington Times it was " a journey into funky thrash , perfect for late night raw energy." To Kerrang! it was "stylish... irresistible... punishing."

What the majority of reviewers missed, however, was that 'Mother's Milk's greatest inspiration was Hillel Slovak. The music and lyrics was deeply infused with the memory of their friend. It was Hillel's painting of the reclining nude which decorated the album's rear sleeve. It was Hillel who had inspired Anthony Kiedis to pen the record's first single – 'Knock Me Down'. It was written for Hillel, about Hillel, and about Anthony's resolve. "If you see me getting high, if you see me getting high, then knock me down..."

92

"I know Hillel would be proud of it," he later said. "And that makes me feel really good. There's also the possibility that wherever he is, he's heard this record and he's getting off on it."

Praise was also heaped on the young shoulders of John Frusciante. Guitar Player hailed him as "a living archive of '70s metal and funk riffs."

There were references to the Chili Peppers' close circle of friends in 'Good Time Boys' and 'Punk Rock Classic'. 'Johnny Kick A Hole In The Sky' was dedicated to America's aboriginal heritage. The Chili Peppers' own tribute to the outstanding LA Lakers' basketball star ('Magic Johnson') was included because, as Kiedis commented, "he is like our music. He flows and glides across the court. So much style."

There was also sufficient sauce ('Sexy American Maid') and pumping histrionics ('Nobody Weird Like Me') to keep the faithful hardcore aficionados sated. Even the front cover (depicting a graceful naked beauty cradling the four Peppers in her arms, the figure of Kiedis deftly covering her right nipple whilst a rose obscured the left!) was said to have been inspired by a local record company rep who accompanied the band on a short promotional visit to Holland.

The Red Hot Chili Peppers had been forced to grow up and confront the death of Hillel through their music. This, however, did not mean that they had to wrap their groins in ice. If 'Mother's Milk' was something of an exorcism for Flea and Anthony Kiedis, then it was a successful purification beyond their wildest dreams.

"We poured our hearts and souls into this record," said Flea. "It's a really honest portrayal of our feelings. I don't know if our vision is more focussed, but the thing about the Red Hot Chili Peppers is that we really mean what we say, and we say it in a way that no other band does."

'Knock Me Down' made it to Number Four on the Billboard chart. EMI released the album on August 28, 1989. When it happened, it happened fast. It had taken a little over six years, the band would often joke like so many before and since, for the Red Hot Chili Peppers to make it as the next 'overnight sensation'.

Chapter 10

The girl in the bikini didn't really know where to hide her face. Yet it was her bottom which presented the most obvious attraction. She had been up-ended over Flea's shoulder and the MTV cameras were everywhere. It was sufficiently humiliating for the girl in the bikini to sue the Red Hot Chili Peppers for sexual battery through the Daytona courts.

It was not the first legal judgement to be meted out by the courts during the band's 50 state live campaign, as they rode high on the wave of 'Mother's Milk'. In retrospect, however, it was certainly the most farcical.

MTV's Spring Break TV Party was the music station's annual back-slapping jamboree conducted in front of live cameras and featuring the uncoolest collection of middle-class jerkies as an audience. It was held on Florida's Daytona Beach. The Red Hot Chili Peppers were asked to mime 'Knock Me Down' for the occasion. The band, they insisted, did not 'mime'. But MTV simply didn't have the facilities for an amplified performance and the band were loath to turn down such exposure. Instead, the Red Hot Chili Peppers agreed to perform the song but only if they could make it blatantly obvious that they were miming. In other words, they would play the game but they would cheat. It was a common enough tactic to somehow escape the patronising ordeal with at least a vestige of credibility intact.

The Spring Break was staged on March 16, 1990. The Red Hot Chili Peppers were months into a heavy schedule and looking forward to letting off a little steam on the beach. Events, however, got out of hand.

Flea was being carried around on Anthony's shoulders when the bassist lost his balance. It was unfortunate for Flea that when he fell, he crashed into a member of the audience. He ended up in the sand with the girl in the bikini sprawled alongside him. 'Knock Me Down' was still booming out of the playback system. Instinctively, Flea jumped up, helped the girl to her feet and threw her arse-first over his shoulder. Witnessing this unscheduled disaster before him, Chad Smith then decided to spank the girl's bottom. It was all intended as one huge joke. It was not a good move.

Two days later, Daytona beach rangers caught up with Flea and Chad Smith. Choosing not to accept Flea's sincerest apologies and put the whole thing down to irresponsible high spirits, the girl opted to prosecute. On August 6, County Judge Freddie Worthen fined Flea and Chad $1000 each (plus a further $300 costs), and ordered both of them to write letters of apology to their 'victim'.

More damaging to the Red Hot Chili Peppers, however, was a case hanging heavy over Anthony Kiedis' head. Charges stemmed from an incident after one show during the band's short tour to break in Chad Smith. The gig at the George Mason University Patriot Centre in Fairfax, Virginia, had been a highlight.

The band were relaxing and recovering backstage when a student volunteer knocked on the dressing room door. She had earlier been appointed as the band's driver. When she appeared that night, Anthony Kiedis allegedly asked her if she had come to "suck my dick".

The girl said she had come to do no such thing. She just wanted to know how long the band would be so she could arrange for the van to pick them up. Laughing, Kiedis nonetheless dropped his sports pants and pointed to his crotch.

The next day, the band discovered that a backstage onlooker had filed misdemeanour charges against Kiedis of indecent exposure and sexual battery. He was stunned to learn that the witness had sworn he had dangled his manhood in her face and had actually touched her with it.

"I'm not that type of person," he rather primly told Kerrang! magazine. "I was changing, and there was a girl there. We were all joking and laughing together and when she left, no-one was under the impression that she was perturbed by my nudity in the dressing room."

The court in Virginia, however, did not agree. Anthony Kiedis was fined $1000 on each count of indecent exposure and sexual battery.

The ramifications of these two court cases would dog the Red Hot Chili Peppers' career forever. The success of 'Knock Me Down' and the subsequent single (a suitably-Peppered version of Stevie Wonder's 'Higher Ground') meant that many new fans of the band were discovering the three previous albums. The unfavourable court judgements, coupled to such ancient songs as 'Party On Your Pussy' and 'Catholic School Girls Rule', resulted in the media establishment painting an infinitely more dubious picture than was actually the case.

According to Flea, the band's reputation affected the courts' verdict. He does, however, admit that the band were not entirely blameless.

"I remember picking the girl up," he told Rolling Stone's David Fricke, "and as far as I was concerned she was thrilled as hell. I didn't know that Chad had spanked her, which was faux pas number one. And in spinning her around I committed a huge faux pas. That is what I really shouldn't have done.
"I did verbally abuse her and that was wrong. I will admit to that every time. I wish I'd never done it, and it was a really stupid thing to do. I was out of control. But I did not abuse anybody, and it was not sexual. It had nothing to do with sex."

REDHOTCHILIPEPPERS
SUGARANDSPICE

"They totally tried to make an example of us," adds Chad Smith.

It was a mark of the Red Hot Chili Peppers' escalating status that the girl who lodged the complaint against Anthony Kiedis would later try unsuccessfully to sue him for $4 million in 1992, claiming that the shock of the events had left her traumatised and mentally scarred.

With typical British irreverence, Rock Pool magazine wondered aloud, "how ugly a willy has to be before you're entitled to $4 million just for seeing it?"

Despite the unmitigated success of the 'Mother's Milk' tour, the Red Hot Chili Peppers would have to fight for their right to party. The Daily News' Jim Farber, for example, rounded on recent litigation when he was charged to review the 'Positive Mental Octopus' video compilation.

"The Chili Peppers take more lusty pleasure in their own bodies than any other band I have ever seen," he wrote. "While it's common for bands to use their flesh to turn on the audience, the Peppers seem more concerned with turning on themselves and each other.

"Members frequently paw their bandmates, or at least pretend to. Singer Anthony fingers the instrument of bassist Flea, moving his fingers up and down the neck whilst Flea writhes in ecstasy. In the concept clip for 'True Men Don't Kill Coyotes', Anthony and Flea press bodies together and mock-kiss, and in the live 'Sexy American Maid', Anthony seizes guitarist John Frusciante and plants a smack on his lips.

"Considering the Peppers' status as avowed heterosexuals, these actions smack of gay-baiting."

The situation rapidly developed into something of a minor witch-hunt. Only when Farber openly accused the band of homophobia, however, were the Chili Peppers forced to commit themselves.

"There's such a wave of red-neck right wing morality sweeping the country," Flea said. "People have said we were sexist for singing 'Party On Your Pussy', or for Anthony making blatantly sexual gestures. But if sex is important to someone, they should sing about it. I see nothing wrong with idolising female genitalia, but just because we like it, it doesn't mean we're homophobic.

"The relationship between music and sex is there to begin with. And the relationship between sex and funk music is even more pronounced. To deny that correlation is preposterous. We're young men and sex is a very important part of our lives. It only makes sense that we would express that in our music."

The Red Hot Chili Peppers rapidly became very bored with this line of antagonism.

"It's very one-dimensional of these people to think that this is the sole basis of what we say and what we play," Anthony told What's On's Danny Scott. "It's only one element. If that's all they can relate to, then maybe their minds are in the gutter. The fact that there is a supremely potent sexual energy in our music is the most natural thing in the world for us and we don't feel any need to curtail that."

These two prosecutions, however, could not overshadow the fact that the 'Mother's Milk' tour was the Chili Peppers' most successful long-haul trek to date. It finally touched down at the sold-out, 6,000 capacity Long Beach arena in Los Angeles.

Maybe, people secretly figured out, the new generation of MTV addicts simply did not care for a band's criminal record. If anything, maybe it made that particular band more appealing as the decade closed. The fact that the Red Hot Chili Peppers could now sport a rap sheet – no matter for what offence – was proof that rock'n'roll bands could still be outlaws. To be seen to ride roughshod over everyday moral constraints was as appealing in 1989 as it had been in 1959 and will be in 1999. To all teenage nobodies in Hellfuck, USA, any band who could fire the Establishment into such a state of apoplectic indignation could indeed rule the world.

The '80s were at an end. The decade which had begun with punk's final clarion call was wheezing into history. It had been a pretty inconsequential decade. The '80s closed with Phil Collins' 'Another Day In Paradise'; a balding multi-millionaire contemplating the homeless situation in Great Britain. It was the perfect empty gesture for an emptier decade.

Yet the escalating success of such new gods as Metallica, Faith No More, Slayer and the Red Hot Chili Peppers was proof that once again the mainstream was badly out of synch with its intended target audience. The Chili Peppers audience wanted to see socks and cocks. They didn't want to see Eric Clapton.

The 'Mother's Milk' tour continued to rage through America's northern states and up into Canada. The sock routine had been largely retired. Yet in Green Bay the stunt made a reappearance, with predictable results.

"*It's very one-dimensional of these people to think that this is the sole basis of what we say and what we play, it's only one element. If that's all they can relate to, then maybe their minds are in the gutter.*"

100

REDHOTCHILIPEPPERS
SUGARANDSPICE

REDHOTCHILIPEPPERS
SUGARANDSPICE

The local security tried to arrest Anthony Kiedis for indecent exposure. The singer bravely denied that he was even in the Red Hot Chili Peppers. It took the combined diplomacy of Lindy Goetz – who had to assure the security crews that the band wore G-strings under the socks and that everything was held in place by tiny wires anyway (untrue but effective!) – and the local police who wisely opted not to pursue the matter further.

There were unscheduled performances elsewhere. Whilst driving through the Canadian Rockies and inspired by the scenery, the band decided to use their mobile generators to power a roadside concert. Passing motorists simply stopped, wound down their windows, and enjoyed the jam like it was a drive-in rock show. It was a good-natured impulse, and reflected the band's own personal state of mind.

The Red Hot Chili Peppers saw in the new decade in San Diego as special guests to the B-52's at Sports Arena. It was a painful show for Kiedis, who sprained his ankle attempting to pole-vault over a microphone stand.
By the time they wound up back home in Los Angeles, the Red Hot Chili Peppers were limping, happy and guilty. Most of all, they were established.

Chapter 11

The tour schedules and impending business confrontations had affected the Red Hot Chili Peppers. Life on the road for the band was invigorating and seldom dull. There were always distractions if anybody was prepared to look hard enough. Yet when the band returned to LA, it was obvious that private relationships were not working out as well.

Flea and Loesha had been battling hard to save a marriage constantly interrupted by lengthy periods of enforced separation. Flea insists that the inevitable outcome was entirely amicable. Certainly, the arrangements for baby Clara seem to enforce this. Flea would be allowed to see his daughter for three days a week when he was off the road. He would not, however, be able to erase the memory of his marriage quite so easily. He still has Loesha's name tattooed on one nipple.

Anthony Kiedis' personal life was also left in tatters when actress Ione Skye traded him in for the Beastie Boys' Adam Horowitz. Anthony and Ione had officially been an item for three years. They met at a party to precede the launch of 'The Uplift Mofo Party Plan', and the singer had once described the daughter of '60s' folk hero Donovan as "one of the most angelic creatures on earth".

Ione had helped Anthony through Hillel's death and the subsequent near-collapse of the Red Hot Chili Peppers. Now that the band had risen from the ashes and flourished way beyond everybody's expectations, Ione felt that it was time to move on. Her own career had started to blossom with recognised roles in both Shock Wave and Johnny Reardon, the latter alongside River Phoenix.

The split would both affect and inspire Anthony. "I will probably miss her for the rest of my life," he admitted.

Despite a growing impression that the continent was dead from the crotch up, the 'Mother's Milk' tour hit Europe in good spirits.

"Germany is not my favourite country in Europe," Anthony told Vox magazine. "But, then again, neither is England. I just find both countries sort of unappealing, sort of bland and not that warm or welcoming. I feel much more comfortable in Holland or Paris. I'm not sure why.

"England is kind of like a giant biscuit, it doesn't change much in taste or texture wherever you are. Though I always look forward to rocking there, that's one thing, especially in places like London. It's good to rock the fuck out there."

REDHOTCHILIPEPPERS
SUGARANDSPICE

"We've always liked music for the reasons of human expression which comes from soul," adds Flea, "and not for like stupid haircuts and shit like that. That's what it's like in England."

"The English music scene sucks. It's terrible. Every time I go over there I'm appalled. If you don't fit into the current trend there then you're out. I think that's really lame."

At the time, however, the Red Hot Chili Peppers wisely kept these thoughts to themselves. The reviews of the British shows overflowed with unbridled enthusiasm for this latest re-incarnation.

"Rabble-rousing honchos with neon rainbows on their bare chests and their fingers in the air," wrote Kerrang!'s Phil Wilding, of the band's show at London's Astoria.

In Amsterdam, all four members of the Chili Peppers returned to Henky Penky's Tattoo Museum for the first time in 18 months. Anthony Kiedis spent most of the afternoon on his stomach, as the artist carefully added to the giant eagle totem which had already taken over the singer's back. Flea, John and Chad all opted for less time-consuming decorations.

Also in that famous European centre of legalised drugs and vice, the band went on a walk-about in full view of Rolling Stone journalist Jeffrey Resner.
"I did some despicable acts," Chad Smith reportedly admitted.

Anthony was vaguer. "Chad definitely had his bizarre behaviour patterns!"
The Red Hot Chili Peppers returned to LA in April 1990, to face their future. The band had become a business as well as a career. Much of their jokey irreverence had been swept into oblivion following Hillel's death and both Flea and Anthony had keen survival instincts. It was time to renegotiate.

"I think selling music is beautiful," Flea admitted. "Sure, art is a totally spiritual thing that you regurgitate just from living, thinking and breathing. But this is a business world. We make records and videos to promote our products so we can drive around on tour buses, make money, and then come home and swim in our pools!"

As the band relaxed beside their swimming pools – a joke reference to the Hollywood celebrity nirvana which all four Chili Peppers eschewed – Lindy Goetz was fielding a succession of heated telephone calls from interested record labels.

It was no secret on the grapevine that the Red Hot Chili Peppers were happy to discuss the possibility of recording for another company after just four albums for EMI. 'Mother's Milk' had turned gold status in North America, and yet both Goetz and the band felt that EMI had never really understood the Red Hot Chili

Peppers' manifesto. A major stumbling block had been the label's refusal to release 'Behind The Sun' as a single from 'The Uplift Mofo Party Plan' in 1988.

This, however, was a purely commercial decision.

EMI had been behind the band since Year Zero. No-one could dispute the label's support throughout the lean years of quiet sales, and the fact that the company had never interfered with either the writing or recording process. They still had the legal right to expect a further three albums under the terms of the original contract. Yet the band felt that it was time to jump ship in order to progress.

Anthony was typically verbose. "We knew the record we were about to make was going to be the greatest piece of music we had ever compiled, and EMI simply wasn't deserving of us. They had always sucked in the past, they were always dropping the ball, coming up short on a regular basis. There was no way we wanted to pour our lives into a record and give it to this inept company. So we decided to look for a company that was more competent and more musically connected."

It was Lindy Goetz's job to extricate the band from this position and find the Red Hot Chili Peppers an alternative home. It was a painstaking process, but one that would eventually prove to be startlingly easy to resolve.

In the meantime, however, the band remained more than active. All four members were quick to travel down to the Memphis studio in which ex-Thelonius Monster's Bob Forrest was recording a solo record ('Beautiful Mess') for RCA. For John Frusciante, it was an honour. Without Forrest, he would never have become a full-on Chili Pepper. Ultimately, the four Peppers spent a great deal of time hanging around and enjoying the vibe.

Flea rented out his talents to rapper Young MC, whilst Anthony busied himself playing a Nazi surf punk in Patrick Swayze's Point Break movie. In July the whole band recorded a version of Bachman Turner Overdrive's 'other' classic – 'Takin' Care Of Business' – as the title track of the impending Jim Belushi film. In October, the Red Hot Chili Peppers kept silent about their ancient anti-charity song recorded for 'Freaky Styley' ('Millionaires Against Hunger), and willingly lined up alongside a further 26 Californian artists to lend their support to LIFE, the LA charity which provided a valuable lifeline to the city's homeless population. It was, the band claimed, because LIFE operated solely in this particular city that they were keen to co-operate. Unlike the global, star-studded Band Aid collaboration, Love Is For Feeding Everyone centred on the Red Hot Chili Peppers' own doorstep. To this day, Anthony Kiedis still actively and relatively quietly helps the homeless with absolutely no desire for publicity. His father told journalist Kim Neely that on Thanksgiving Day, Anthony bought 50 meals and distributed them himself amongst the LA vagrants.

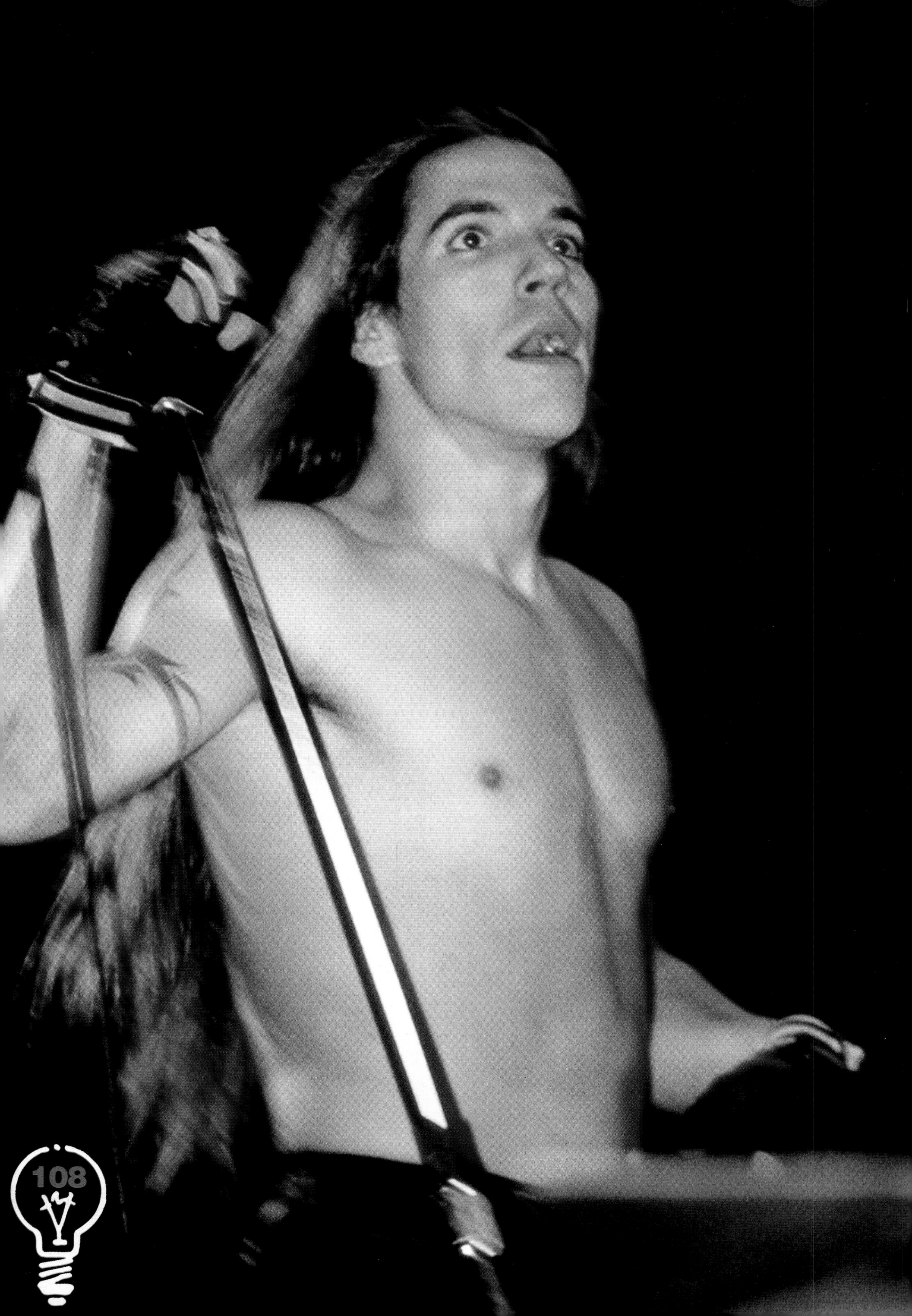

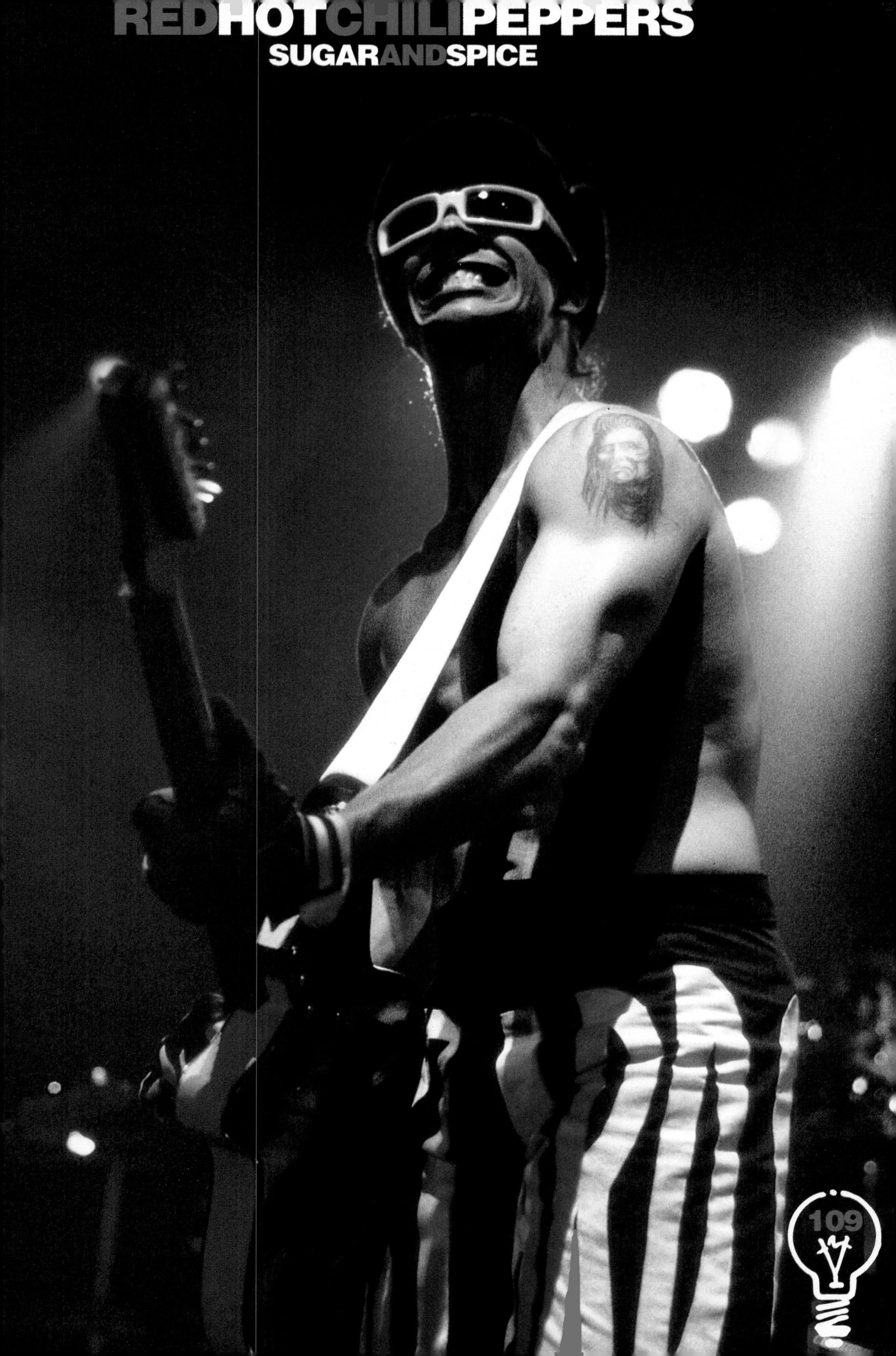

"With little placemats," Blackie Dammett added. "He designed them and signed them and everything. He does that kind of stuff all the time, but he'd never tell you about it."

In the evenings, the four Chili Peppers spent their time at parties thrown in their honour by the ever-growing list of corporate suitors. They had managed to buy their way out of the contract with EMI for an undisclosed sum. Lindy Goetz was negotiating like a Wall Street veteran, playing every label off against another and generally stirring up a hornet's nest of interest. It was not difficult to peddle the Red Hot Chili Peppers' particular potential.

Eventually the bidding came down to two labels – Sony Music subsidiary Epic, and the massive Warner Brothers corporation. Regrettably, they had turned down everyone else including Rick Rubin's Def American label. Rubin, however, had been offered another opportunity to produce the Red Hot Chili Peppers' next album as a consolation prize. Rubin had graciously accepted this offer.

Said Goetz on his final decision: "Epic Records offered us more money than we thought was humanly possible!"

The contracts were drawn up for the band by lawyer Eric Greenspan, and returned to Epic for one final approval. The band had their photograph taken with the label's president.

Everyone, it seemed, had under-estimated the resolve of Warner's chairman, Mo Ostin.

Anthony, Flea, John and Chad were all at home when they each received a call from Ostin. Mo Ostin, the man who had signed Jimi Hendrix, Neil Young and Emmylou Harris to Warners, personally called the Red Hot Chili Peppers to wish them good luck with their new label and to assure the band that he harboured no hard feelings.

"The fucking chairman of Warners calls a lowly fucking band guy to wish us luck!" Chad Smith remembers thinking. "A real class act!"

Anthony Kiedis was similarly shocked and began to reconsider the situation. "I was touched by his humaneness. It really made me feel that maybe Warner Brothers was the place we would feel more at home."

The band told Goetz to tear up the Epic contract. The label was furious but since nothing had been officially signed they were also powerless.

Warner Brothers bought the Red Hot Chili Peppers for around $7 million. A real class act indeed.

Anthony Kiedis had no real reason to feel depressed. The Red Hot Chili Peppers' future spread out before the singer like a sunny weekend. With Chad and John now firmly established as legitimate Peppers, the band Kiedis and Flea had started all those years ago as a joke finally seemed complete. They had the accolades and shiny gold discs to prove their success.

Yet Anthony Kiedis was feeling uncharacteristically morose. Wrenched from the comforting bosom of a stable relationship, the singer felt in a state of limbo. He felt like he had no-one outside the band with whom to enjoy the fruits of his labour.

"I was driving away from the rehearsal studio," he told David Fricke, "and thinking how I just wasn't making any connection with my friends or family, I didn't have a girlfriend, and Hillel (Slovak) wasn't there. The only thing I could grasp was this city.

"I grew up here for the last twenty years, and it was LA – the hills, the buildings, the people in it as a whole – that seemed to be looking out for me more than any human being. I just started singing this little song to myself.

"When I got home that day, I started thinking about my life and how sad it was right now. But no matter how sad or lonely I got, things were a million percent better than they were two years earlier when I was using drugs all the time. There was no comparison. I was reminding myself 'Okay, things might feel fucked up right now, but I don't ever want to feel like I did two years ago.'

"Epic Records offered us more money than we thought was humanly possible!"

"In the end it wasn't like I was writing in any sort of pop song format. I just started writing about the bridge – and the things that occurred under the bridge."

It was a lonely, desperate situation that would inspire the Red Hot Chili Peppers' most successful hit single. The particular bridge in question, Kiedis told Rolling Stone magazine, had to remain a secret.

"It's down-town," he says. "I don't want people looking for it. You had to be family to go there. That was just one of the predicaments I found myself in, the kind that only drug addiction can bring about. That's just one day that sticks very vividly in my mind."

The Red Hot Chili Peppers were in pre-production with Rick Rubin for 'BloodSugarSexMagik' when Anthony Kiedis first mentioned 'Under The Bridge'. Rick Rubin was intrigued and persuaded Anthony to sing it to him. The song, he knew, was the first sign that this record was not going to be a typical Chili Peppers' affair. It was going to be special.

"It ('Under The Bridge') doesn't really have a hook," Chad Smith later explained. "And not to take anything away from Anthony, but he's not the greatest singer in the world. It's just cool and soulful. It's not the like the guy who wins all the awards – Michael Bolton – but maybe that's why it's so great."

As ever, the environment had to be ideal for the Chili Peppers to sound 'cool and soulful'. As Flea said: "You can go into some bitchin' recording studio and for all you know, Poison or some stupid shit was on the tape player before you were. Can you imagine going on a machine that had the vibe of Poison on it and trying to do something cool? That's sick, man!"

It was Rick Rubin's idea to move the Red Hot Chili Peppers – cock, stock and barrel – into a rented house out in Laurel Canyon. It had no telephone. The electricity would have to be re-connected. But Rubin saw the house as a sanctuary from the craziness of Los Angeles. Moving every gadget – from the lowliest plugboard to the recording desk itself – into the secluded house would be like building a page of history.

The band, remembering how boring their time at George Clinton's farmhouse had been, were initially reluctant. Yet Rubin talked further and finally the band agreed.

"The best thing I did to prepare for this record," Flea later said, "was to lose my phone book and break my foot! That helped me concentrate. I had no contact with anyone for a couple of months."

There were enough stories concerning the house to keep an army of triviologists content. Built in 1917, it was a huge, bare-walled hacienda with naked floorboards and an old piano. It was said that previous occupants included Rudolph Valentino, Harry Houdini, Jimi Hendrix and the Beatles. There were said to be a network of underground tunnels once used by smugglers in the Prohibition-era, and everyone was convinced that some of these occupants had never actually left the house at all.

"There are definitely ghosts in the house," John Frusciante commented. "But they are very friendly. We have nothing but warm vibes and happiness everywhere we go in this house."

Two psychics, however, tried to scare the current occupants by saying that the house stifled creativity, and then demanded money.

"If I see them again," Frusciante muttered, "I think I will just hit them in the face." The psychics, however, did stress that a room on the second floor had a strong sexual vibe. Frusciante was not ashamed to admit that he had masturbated in the room. "I actually heard a woman being fucked in there."

But Flea's four-year-old daughter loved the house, and left her mark on the walls with indelible biro. John Frusciante decorated his room with a few paintings, as Rick Rubin began assembling a heap of machinery in the spacious living room. It was essentially a mess of wires.

"The best thing I did to prepare for this record, was to lose my phone book and break my foot! That helped me concentrate. I had no contact with anyone for a couple of months."

The bear-like producer was finally ready. "If it's not here," he told the band, "then you can't have it, because you don't need it. And don't be thinking that if you make any mistakes, you can just go back and erase them later."

The band hired the services of an ex-Playboy model as a cook, who spent all day listening to a radical, militant radio station. They reluctantly had to fire a security guard because he couldn't be budged from his Nintendo games' console. Essentially, the Red Hot Chili Peppers winched up the drawbridge, bolted the doors, and let nobody hear anything until 'BloodSugarSexMagik' was virtually complete.

The only time they ventured far from their hi-tec flop house was to record a version of Robert Johnson's 'They're Red Hot' on the hills overlooking the freeway at 2am.

The album took two months to record and mix. It would last the Red Hot Chili Peppers the best part of three years.

Chapter 12

 nthony Kiedis was adamant. "I know that we've made a record that has inspired us to stay together for many years. If we can make something this great there's no telling what the future holds."

BloodSugarSexMagik' was released in September 1991 to unanimous critical acclaim. It was a busy week for the major labels. Nirvana's 'Nevermind' and Guns N'Roses' double 'Use Your Illusion' set competed for dollars, but the Red Hot Chili Peppers' record would eventually clock up sales in excess of 2 million. "It's as sure-footed a groove as they could possibly strike," wrote Mike Gitter. "Trailing off into a rainbow of new directions. A brighter, louder explosion of colours delivered with love and glowing sensual warmth."

It was the record that the band had always boasted they could deliver. It was a record built on the energies of sadness, strength, harmony and horniness. It was the ultimate melting pot.

The sex ('Sir Psycho Sexy', 'Funky Monks' and 'Suck My Kiss') earned the record the by now almost standard Parental Advisory stickers. The sadness ('My Lovely Man' and 'Under The Bridge') merited Kiedis a more mature reputation for his sincerity.

As he told David Fricke: "Especially living in the city of Los Angeles and doing what I do, it's very easy to get wrapped up like an onion with millions of layers of bullshit and completely lose touch with your inner core. You forget you're just a person with these real feelings of love and sadness and happiness and horniness and pleasure. You just kind of go through life like a rolling fucking snowball, picking up more layers as you go along. Every now and then, I need to get reminded that I'm just a person with these feelings.

"Hillel reminds me. More than anything else in the world Hillel reminds me.

"The other day, I was going through this thing where I've got about forty appointments and I'm answering a million phone calls and opening letters and packages, and I got this package in the mail from this girl who's been a friend of mine for years, who had been holding onto this little box for me, this little brown-paper box which Hillel had given me in 1986. There was something written on the box, and it said: 'Anthony, you think what I feel and understand what I say. I love you. This is our year, 24. Hillel.'

"I went out into my back yard, and I just sat there for a minute. And all of a sudden, I managed to get through all of those layers, and I got to the real me. I started crying and talking to myself – and talking to Hillel.

115

"'My Lovely Man' is about my love for Hillel and the feeling that eventually I will find him. It's kind of like when I die, I am counting on him to save me a seat. And whenever I sing that song, Hillel is completely in my world."

This was a new Anthony Kiedis talking. This was the Anthony Kiedis who cycled 50 kilometres for an interview to promote 'BloodSugarSexMagik'. This was the Anthony Kiedis who would rave about endomorphines and maple syrup. This was the Anthony Kiedis whose one remaining vice was cigarettes. This was the Anthony Kiedis who would accompany Madonna on a version of Frank Sinatra's 'The Lady Is A Tramp' for the Arsenio Hall Show wearing stockings, a little black dress and a huge grin. This was the bright, new, shiny Anthony Kiedis.

The first single to be lifted from the album was 'Give It Away'. The polished, proto-bump was a typical slug of Chili Peppers, and released by Warners in a bid to hook the hardcore fanbase. With the band's new-found status, there was perhaps a feeling that fans of the old material would have been disturbed by Kiedis' recent talk of dead friends and brotherly love. 'Give It Away' was a trailblazer for the album.

It was also a song to encompass neatly the point of the Red Hot Chili Peppers. "What I've got you've got to put in you," Kiedis scat-rapped lasciviously, only to lament the "Greedy little people in sea of distress" elsewhere.

But most importantly, strippers could dance to 'Give It Away'. It was never far from the radio or MTV, hammering its hooks into the public psyche and proving to be something of yardstick for the booming funk metal scene. In 1993 this was recognised by MTV as 'Give It Away' was awarded Best Hard Rock Track With Vocal in 1992.

"I know that we've made a record that has inspired us to stay together for many years. If we can make something this great there's no telling what the future holds."

It was, however, 'Under The Bridge' itself which attracted the mainstream to the Red Hot Chili Peppers. Released whilst 'BloodSugarSexMagik' was still fresh on the shelves, Anthony Kiedis' gentle and harrowing exorcism oozed through to a willing worldwide audience. The fact that it was adopted as a classic smooch by loving suburban couples did not matter. Anthony Kiedis had at least lain several ghosts to rest in style.

REDHOTCHILIPEPPERS
SUGARANDSPICE

Rolling Stone described 'Under The Bridge' as "an impressive fluke. They have finally scored commercially with a nervy slice of melodrama that is streets away from mosh-ville."

Anthony Kiedis reacted mischievously to the song's success. "What kills me," he said, "is that there are so many people getting into 'Under The Bridge' across America who have no idea what the Chili Peppers are like. Take a group of Kansas housewives who turn on the radio and say: 'Oh, I like that sweet, sentimental song. Honey, would you go out and get me this record?' They get the record, and there's 'Sir Psycho Sexy' and 'The Power Of Equality'. They are going to have their little world turned upside down.

"I have this wonderful image of this lady washing the dishes in her little home in Kansas with her little tape deck, popping this in and taking off her clothing, running into the back yard and getting loosed up a bit!"
The song bolted into the Billboard Top 10 and hung around for eight weeks. By this time the Red Hot Chili Peppers were back on the road and headlining a package that many were tipping to be the most successful in 1992.
Here we are now... entertain us.

Nirvana joined the Red Hot Chili Peppers' tour in December 1991 – the same month that they released a single which would ultimately alter the way music was perceived, delivered and marketed for years to come. 'Smells Like Teen Spirit' was not just four chords of nonsense and a perfect vocal. Nirvana's debut single from their first major label album ('Nevermind') was the flood-gatekeeper.

Suddenly grunge was a talking point for chat shows, tabloid newspapers and teen magazines. The fashion industry lumbered up to kiss grunge's asshole. Supermodels dressed down to get noticed. Movie stars looked like vagabonds and aspiring dollar brokers hacked off the pony-tails and let their hair grow to the required grunge length – one inch longer than fucking stupid.

Nirvana allegedly hated the song and the subsequent repercussions. It was a dumb song that made no sense. Yet it was ideal for the times. It was cynical and funny and hungry and bored. It raged and wept and shrieked about nothing very much. Millions, however, took it to heart. They pumped their pennies and cents into jukeboxes to hear Kurt Cobain's voice cut across the lush sonic arrangement like a dentist's drill. It was a huge breath of fresh air and it signalled a media frenzy that would eventually drive Kurt Cobain to blow his brains out with a shotgun in 1994.

To the army of fans who remembered 'Bleach' (Nirvana's first and considerably under-produced debut album), and Mudhoney, and Green River, and Ten Minute Warning, and The Replacements, and Skin Yard – all pioneers of the local underground movement that the media dubbed grunge – 'Smells Like Teen Spirit' probably killed the whole scene. It became 'Bat Out Of Hell'.

117

REDHOTCHILIPEPPERS
SUGARANDSPICE

'Nevermind' became an album that the 30-somethings simply had to have on CD. Grunge stopped being a teenager following '...Teen Spirit's success.

By the time Nirvana hooked up with the Red Hot Chili Peppers that December, 'Nevermind' had been in the shops for two months. It was selling at a rate of 70,000 copies a day, and during the week that the tour started it finally toppled Michael Jackson's 'Thriller' from the top of the Billboard Album Charts.

By the time the tour reached San Francisco on New Year's Eve, Pearl Jam were opening the evening. If ever a new era in music was born, it was this package on New Year's Eve at the 'Frisco Oakland Coliseum. Not only was it a whole new attitude for the music industry to grasp, not only was it the sound of something urgent and thrilling – up there with bleeding hearts and painstaking souls, but also proof that this was a total commercial victory as well.

The Red Hot Chili Peppers and Nirvana had little in common musically. Yet both bands came from a staunch underground movement which had started in basements and bars and garages and bedrooms. Both bands believed in getting something started, recruiting like-minded associates and trying to survive by listening to each others' hearts. The fact that the results would become a fashion was almost insulting.

It was not a good time to be in an adult orientated rock band with big hair and leather trousers. The LA metal circuit was finally losing its stranglehold as the main players grew little beards and learnt to de-tune their shiny metal guitars.

Irony was a whole new concept for the dumbo rockers to master. Harley Davidsons were out and battered pick-ups were in. Some were not slow to ditch their past and re-invent themselves as sensitive artists with poetry books replacing porno books, messages replacing massage parlours and coffee replacing cocaine.

It was, finally, the perfect time to be a Red Hot Chili Pepper.

Chapter 13

BloodSugarSexMagik' was officially certified Platinum (sales of over one million) in April 1992. 'Under The Bridge' would soon peak at Number Two, and the Red Hot Chili Peppers were eastern-bound for a sold-out tour of Japan and Australia. Flea was going home. Everyone was a little on edge. It was unchartered territory for the band.

John Frusciante's moods were put down to youth, temperament, shyness and the workload. He was not an easy interview for the world's Press. Neither a natural extrovert nor social performer, John Frusciante was just 21 and already feeling the strain. He was, in fact, utterly frustrated at the spotlight constantly picking out his physique, his hair, his tattoos... anything except his guitar playing.

"So many people miss the point with us," he told BAM magazine. "They copy the thumb slapping or the silly faces, but they miss the essence of what we really are. Every time I read something about what we are, it completely misses the point. We're trying to tap into all the good vibes in the universe and yet all we ever see is 'cocks-in-socks'. It's ridiculous."

It was typical of Frusciante that in 1991, whilst on a promotional trip to London, he simply woke up, decided he couldn't face another bout of useless questions, and flew home.

The Red Hot Chili Peppers made a fatal mistake when they presumed that John Frusciante was merely sensitive and sometimes just a little too creative for his own good. In Japan they finally discovered how wrong they had been. On the afternoon of May 7, Anthony Kiedis was on the telephone talking to a reporter in New Zealand when Flea walked into the singer's hotel room. Anthony remembers that Flea looked "puzzled, sad, surreal".

Flea blurted out the bombshell, telling Anthony that John Frusciante wanted to leave the band and he wanted to leave the band right now. Tonight. Forever.

"The news stunned me and it shattered me," Anthony later admitted. "I could tell by the look in John's eyes that he was really serious. He said 'I can't stay in the band anymore. I've reached a state where I can't do justice to what we've created, because of stress and fatigue. I can't give what it takes to be in this band any more.'"

The Red Hot Chili Peppers knew that nothing any of them could say would persuade their friend and guitarist to stay. It was over.

Lindy Goetz, perhaps visualising the small army of promoters and agents who would be after the band's blood when informed of the cancelled shows, tentatively asked John Frusciante what he should tell people.

"Just tell everyone I went crazy," he replied, with a shy smile. He agreed to play that evening's show. Then in the morning he got a cab to the airport and flew home. The Red Hot Chili Peppers were once again in total and utter disarray. In retrospect, there had been warning signs. Anthony Kiedis and John Frusciante had communicated little during the past tour. Flea had taken the guitarist out for a stroll in the park and asked if he still enjoyed being in the Red Hot Chili Peppers. Flea, ever the diplomat and not wanting to force a confrontation, tried his best to shield John Frusciante from the combat stress. The truth was that Frusciante simply could not cope with life on the road as a Red Hot Chili Pepper.

"The news stunned me and it shattered me, I could tell by the look in John's eyes that he was really serious. He said 'I can't stay in the band anymore. I've reached a state where I can't do justice to what we've created, because of stress and fatigue. I can't give what it takes to be in this band any more'."

"Part of it was the constant pressure," Flea would later admit. "Given all that goes on with the Red Hot Chili Peppers, it's easy to let the rest of your life fall apart, and I think John needed to take care of his life, his sanity and his peace of mind because it was driving him batty. He needed his space."

No-one at the time, however, could believe Frusciante's decision to quit. "It was perfectly devastating," Anthony later admitted. "It was like catastrophe all over again. We gain a family member after Hillel dying, which was like your heart getting squashed like a grape under a rhino's stomp, and then John comes to us like this great blessing from I don't know where and we all fall in love with him and his creativity. Then my man just snaps and departs.

"Musicians and artists tend to be these crazy, delicate, fucked-up freaks of nature, which I love, but they're susceptible to snaps. John was so young when he joined the band, and then we started getting really popular – which is a strange thing, because the Peppers have always really been an underground commodity. Then the world starts embracing you, and it's kind of a hard thing to deal with in some ways. All that recognition and attention, that's not much especially if you're like this timid weirdo like John was."

The "timid weirdo" himself would remain silent on the subject for three years. For a while John Frusciante did nothing. He kicked back in the sun, played his guitar for his own enjoyment only, and immersed himself in solitude. Then he started to write. He was alone in his house with just his guitars and soul for company, and that was just fine by John Frusciante.

"I had a weird premonition that I should quit immediately after I finished my guitar parts on 'BloodSugar...'," the guitarist told Artie Nelson in RAW magazine, in November 1994.

"I'd say to myself, 'I know you don't have any reason to, but you've gotta quit the band.'

"But I couldn't bring myself to do it, because I knew they wouldn't let me. It wouldn't make sense to them. But I had this feeling that the road was really gonna fuck with me. The road had been fucking with Flea for so many years, and it'd be bad of me to have to quit then, but I was sure I should do it.

"It just had to do with my subconscious and my development as a person and spirit. "I felt like a guy with 400 ghosts telling him what to do all the time. I just wanted to lay back on the couch and think about nothing, and that's what I did till I went on tour, aside from one miserable two week European interview thing.

"The unity hadn't been good with the band for ages. Me and Anthony didn't look at each other much on stage. I told Flea that I was just in the band because I loved him. 'I love playing with you, and I don't want to leave you, but there's nothing I like about being in the band.'

"And he said, 'I guess you shouldn't do it just for me'. He understood, but he didn't think about it for the next year. So when I quit it was a shock. To them, it seemed like it was getting better as far as getting along went. But I didn't want to do it anymore. I was really happy, in outer space every time I would look at Flea's eyes, or my amp, or Chad's foot. But the popularity thing bummed me out.

"It's not like I'm against popularity. When I was 17 and I was at the last Chili Peppers show I ever saw before joining them. Hillel asked me, 'Would you still like the Chilis if they got so popular they played the LA Forum?'

123

"I said, 'No. It would ruin the whole thing that's great about the band. The audience feels no different from the band at all'. There was this real kind of historical vibe at their shows, none of the frustration that runs through the audience when they jump around and can't get out out of their seats. I didn't even watch the shows. I'd get so excited that I'd flip around the slam pit the whole time. I really feel like a part of the band, and all the sensitive people in the audience did too. So I couldn't picture the band playing the LA Forum, and when we got to that point of popularity it bugged me for that and a number of other reasons."

The band toughed out the inevitable consequence of John Frusciante's overnight departure. Anthony Kiedis, particularly, put on a brave face. "We hoped it would work out," he told Rolling Stone. "John was one of the most deeply soulful guitar players that we've ever been connected with. Also, he was a good friend, and we had something going that was cosmic and special. And now we're going to have to find that elsewhere.

"We've got to look at it like, we've got to get someone who is just happier, and just wants to rock equally as hard. There are a couple of people in Hollywood that we greatly admire and revere. We'll get in touch with them and start playing. We're not going to do a massive audition process. We're just going to look at people we know and try to find that chemistry again."

It was a frustrating task. Not only did they have to find a guitar player, they had to find a Red Hot Chili Pepper. Just a mere musician would not be good enough. The candidate had to be a friend and brother.

The two remaining shows in Japan were cancelled. Instead the whole operation headed east for Australia. They had already contacted Zander Schloss, the former Thelonius Monster guitarist and a long-standing Chili Peppers ally. Everyone was aware that it was a long shot. Yet Zander dropped everything and flew out to meet the band for several frantic rehearsals in Australia. No-one, however, was particularly surprised when the giant Chili Peppers motor failed to ignite. Exhausted, drained and resigned, the Red Hot Chili Peppers realised that the Australian shows were going to be an insurmountable battle. They agreed to pull the rest of the tour and reluctantly returned to Los Angeles.

It was perhaps the worst possible time for the band to be looking for a guitarist. Whoever they found would not only have to contribute on the successor to a platinum album, but also debut in North America in front of 40,000 people at the second Lollapalooza festival in July. There was also a high-profile Belgian festival slated in as a warm-up. By the time the Red Hot Chili Peppers had re-grouped in Los Angeles, there were just six weeks to break in a guitarist before they would all have to walk out on stage to headline Perry Farrell's giant celebration of counter-culture. The Chili Peppers were adamant that they would play both festivals. It was a heart-stopping deadline.

REDHOTCHILIPEPPERS
SUGAR AND SPICE

The first Lollapalooza in 1990 was intended as a stylish and varied swansong for Jane's Addiction. It was an inspired but ambitious project, largely conceived by Jane's Addiction's frontman Perry Farrell and drummer Steve Perkins.

Lollapalooza was to all intents and purposes a travelling summer festival, featuring not only the cream of alternative culture but also political information booths and sideshows. It was to be a freak circus; a bedlam.

It was unlike any other North American tour. The usual pomp and ridiculous sterility of the typical stadium environment was replaced by a loose and chaotic mesh of artistic assault. Confirmed for the 26 date, nationwide haul were Siouxsie And The Banshees, Nine Inch Nails, Ice T, Living Colour, Henry Rollins, the Butthole Surfers and Jane's Addiction.

The fact that Lollapalooza eventually came 25th in Performance magazine's list of profitable top tours was all the proof needed by Perry Farrell to consider a second gathering.

The success of the first Lollapalooza convinced many sceptics that the second would be the ultimate tour package. As Anthony Kiedis pointed out, when the Chili Peppers were confirmed as the headline attraction: "If I didn't get off on it so heavily the last time, I wouldn't have been so inclined to be a part of it this year."

It is perhaps understandable that the pressure of finding a new guitarist caused Kiedis to bitch out loud about the looming festival.

He was upset that he could not speak directly to Perry Farrell and was told instead to fax him via the ticket agency. He was also frustrated at the "maleness" of the bill, and fought hard for L7 to be added to the bill to redress the balance.

"I wanted L7 on the bill," he said, "but everybody in the agency just laughed. They said they (L7) didn't mean anything. I said, 'What do you mean? They rock, and they're girls'. It was kind of upsetting for me."

But the Red Hot Chili Peppers could not afford the luxury of direct protest. Instead they had just three weeks to break in John Frusciante's replacement. Ex-Jane's Addiction guitarist, David Navarro, had been top of the band's shortlist. Since Jane's Addiction folded after the first Lollapalooza tour as promised, relations between Navarro and Perry Farrell had been strained. The fact that the two would be re-united for the second Lollapalooza outing was the principal reason for Navarro to decline the Chili Peppers' offer. Anthony, Flea and Chad might just have been consoled by the news that Navarro had also turned down an offer from Axl Rose to join Guns N'Roses.

125

It was a while before Flea remembered a "skinny, blewish kid" he had once jammed with more than two years ago. Flea was on the phone to Arik Marshall before he could even remember how to spell his name.

The two had first run into each other with an itinerant pool of musicians known as Trulio Disgracias. Flea had played trumpet for them whilst limbering up for the 'Mother's Milk' tour. Trulio Disgracias consisted of various members of Fishbone and Thelonius Monster, and Arik was the younger brother of Thelonius Monster's Lonnie Marshall.

"We'd always see one another around different clubs," Arik later explained. "Something of a friendship developed over the years. It was like a mutual admiration thing. Flea and Anthony would come and see my bands and I'd go see theirs."

Flea: "The first time I head Arik Marshall play was in some little club somewhere. I said, 'Okay, this guy's funky' – like he was good, but I wasn't impressed. Next time I heard him play was in Trulio Disgracias, and I said, 'Whoa!'. Then I heard him play with his brother Lonnie in Marshall Law, and it was phenomenal! Amazing! Incredible! Like this psychedelic, liquid, funky trip. I thought, 'This guy is the greatest fucking guitar player!'."

The Red Hot Chili Peppers found Arik playing in a one-off funk troupe (alongside Norwood Fishbone and their old friend Alain Johannes) which had been assembled purely to play a Beverly Hills graduation party. They moved quickly, welcoming Arik Marshall into the bosom of the beast.

"It's been really stressful," Anthony said at the time. "Because if you think about the fact that we've been a band for nine years, trying to get nine years' worth of love and magic and creative exploration into a one-month period is kind of a tall order. But we've found this character, Arik, who's a really beautiful person. That's real important to the band. There's got to be a brotherhood. I mean, we auditioned guitarists that were just mind-boggling, they could play every note imaginable in about three seconds, y'know, but there's more to being a Chili Pepper than being able to play your ass off. It's a belief in what you're doing, being truthful, honest, and having integrity."

Arik Marshall made his public debut in front of 60,000 Belgian festival fans. He would later describe it as "the most, exhilarating and terrifying experience of my life!".

Yet there was no time to dwell on such sensations. The band immediately flew home for Lollapalooza II. It was to be the most important show of strength from a band whose reputation for losing guitarists was starting to precede them. The Red Hot Chili Peppers needed to show North America that the band had not fallen apart. They desperately needed a victory on their home turf.

Lollapalooza II was a commercial triumph which exceeded everybody's expectations. Whether it was an artistic success, however, was less certain. It was an impressive line-up. The likes of Lush, Pearl Jam, Ice Cube, Soundgarden and Ministry all preceded the Red Hot Chili Peppers.

Taking Lollapalooza's diverse ingredients into the belly of white suburban American proved to be a frustrating exercise. The audience drank beer, basked in the sun, tried to get off with the opposite sex and ate a ton of hamburger. It became another rock festival. The stalls offering information on a variety of causes (Rock The Vote, No More Censorship, PETA, American Cannabis Society, Act-Up and AIDS Action Group) were largely overlooked by the middle class rock fans who only knew the Red Hot Chili Peppers for 'Under The Bridge' and Anthony Kiedis' torso. It was perhaps understandable that people flocked to Lollapalooza in their thousands for a good time. They didn't want preachers. They wanted pop stars.

The Red Hot Chili Peppers played from 9.30pm until 11 pm and delivered everything this MTV audience demanded. Flea played in his white baggy underpants, and took time out to sing a haunting, solo rendition of Neil Young's 'The Needle And The Damage Done'. Whether this song meant as much to the crowd as the sight of the whole band wearing helmets which shot jets of flame high up into the lighting gantry, was debatable. To people familiar with the Chili Peppers' history, however, it was a poignant few moments.

> *"We'd always see one another around different clubs, something of a friendship developed over the years. It was like a mutual admiration thing. Flea and Anthony would come and see my bands and I'd go see theirs."*

Journalists visiting the Red Hot Chili Peppers during the sprawling tour found the entourage in buoyant mood. The band were clearly enjoying the success and the celebrity.

"I feel like the President," Flea jokingly told freelance writer Steffan Chirazi. "Kiss that baby!"

"Of course, you get little girls at the airport saying stuff to you like, 'I love your album 'Under The Bridge'. And you know that they only know that one fucking song, but what's so bad about that? All it means is that they'll hopefully get into more of our music.

"There's nothing else to it. We just love the music, have fun doing it, playing it, feeling it. There's no big plan, and there never really has been."

Anthony Kiedis: "That's all part of the foundation that Flea and I have because we've been doing it for so long. We did those Chevy van tours for years, and I suppose it does make it easier to climb that ladder of musical popularity." Some things had never changed. Trip Brown has been the Chili Peppers' agent since the release of 'Freaky Styley'.

"This ain't no overnight success story, y'know," he said. "They've worked damn hard for this, paid their dues and are now reaping their rewards. The band have got to where they are through good old-fashioned legwork, not through company hype. They've played every dive from here to Shitsville probably twice, and every time they play a gig they put in 200%, whether it's to a crowd of 50 or 50,000."

And the rewards were considerable. "Success basically means money," said Flea, "and I have no aversion to success."

Anthony Kiedis admitted that he had been known to spend up to $10,000 on a painting, a passion encouraged by John Frusciante and one that has remained with the singer.

The Lollapalooza tour was the Red Hot Chili Peppers' crowning glory. When it was finally over, the band were to sit back and contemplate their future. Eventually they would start work on their sixth record.

Anthony Kiedis met up with an old friend (Hank Schiffmacher) in Borneo for a hastily-prepared jungle trek.

"We were going to cross the entire island," he said. "It turned into the most harrowing, semi-unpleasant test of survival that I've ever subjected myself to.

"I had these great images of myself swinging from vines and playing in the jungle and finding orang-utan and dancing among exotic flowers. But it turned into more of a Vietnam experience. Everyone got brutally ill. At night, we would sleep in these incredibly uncomfortable, wet, seething-with-jungle-life conditions. The first night in the jungle, we weren't using our mosquito netting, and I woke up with this incredibly painful buzzing and humming inside my brain. I woke up Hank and said: 'Please, look in my ear, my head is vibrating, and I'm going insane'. He's got the flashlight, and he's looking in my ear: 'No, I see nothing, I see nothing'.

128

129

"And then he drops the flashlight and screams and I feel this animal crawl out of my ear. He said it looked like an oversize jungle roach that had somehow collapsed its body and worked its way into my ear canal and gotten stuck.

"This ain't no overnight success story, y'know, they've worked damn hard for this, paid their dues and are now reaping their rewards. The band have got to where they are through good old-fashioned legwork, not through company hype. They've played every dive from here to Shitsville probably twice, and every time they play a gig they put in 200%, whether it's to a crowd of 50 or 50,000."

"So I wasn't having the greatest time. And halfway through, we got lost in these mountains in the middle of Borneo. And when you're a white guy from California, and you've run out of food, and you can't communicate fluently with your guides, it becomes a source of concern.

"Then Flea and I took a trip to Costa Rica. There were lots of high-adventure travelling activities because we knew we were getting ready to make another record."

Chapter 14

 The successor to 'BloodSugarSexMagik' had to be special. When the Red Hot Chili Peppers regrouped early in 1993, they knew that their sixth studio record would have to shine against one of the biggest-selling records of the '90s. It was a difficult task.

Writing began slowly in rehearsals. It was difficult for Flea to get up a head of steam. He felt tired and lethargic. He was driving his old, spray-painted Mercedes to the studio, but nothing was jumping out from the strings. He was plugging in and just running through the motions.

For Arik Marshall it was also a struggle. He had completed the touring schedule and had slotted expertly into the Chili Peppers' brotherhood. Now the spotlight was on his song-writing abilities and it was dazzling. Every riff he came up with seemed to leak. Everyone knew that this great molten heart was not beating correctly. It became a torturous situation. Eventually the strain began to show.

Anthony Kiedis remained the most visible Chili Pepper. His appearance with Madonna on the Arsenio Hall Show and their subsequent embrace, fuelled the rumour-mill and invited speculation. Both parties, however, remained tight-lipped. Kiedis had always been a gentleman, and a gentleman never tells.

Behind the scenes, however, the Red Hot Chili Peppers were grinding to a halt. Flea was finally diagnosed with 'Chronic Fatigue Syndrome' by his doctors, after his uncharacteristic lethargy made rehearsals impossible.

ME, or 'Yuppy Flu' as it was immediately dubbed by the media on discovery, is a stress-related illness which can afflict anybody. It is a sign that the body cannot go on without rest. With the song-writing process proving to be a disappointment, Flea was ordered to rest for three months before returning to the fray.

The news, when it was released to the press in June, was seized upon, dissected, and in several cases interpreted with more colour than care. Some magazines reported that Flea had been ordered to rest for a year. Others speculated on the entire future of the Red Hot Chili Peppers. 'Chilis Split As Flea Burns Out?' was one of the typical British headlines.

Record company spokesmen and women tried to underplay the situation, even though it clearly meant that a European tour and several festival appearances (including headlining appearances at Glastonbury, Sunstroke and Dublin Dalymount Park) would now have to be cancelled. It also meant that the new record would have to be postponed on the schedules.

"Then Flea and I took a trip to Costa Rica. There were lots of high-adventure travelling activities because we knew we were getting ready to make another record."

REDHOTCHILIPEPPERS
SUGARANDSPICE

The last public sighting of the band had been at the Grammys in February, when the Chili Peppers beat the likes of Alice In Chains, Faith No More and Guns N'Roses, for the Best Hard Rock Performance With Vocal award. It would have to be a brave man to bet any money on the Red Hot Chili Peppers splitting up.

Yet press reports that Arik Marshall had been sacked were not so far from the truth. A week after announcing Flea's illness, the Red Hot Chili Peppers confirmed that they were no longer writing with Arik. In fact the band had already advertised in the LA Times for a replacement. The advert had been designed by Flea's daughter, Clara.

"The emotional connection just wasn't there," Anthony Kiedis would later say.

Over 5,000 hopefuls tried to make the required connection. No-one, however, made the grade.

"We were looking for very specific, cosmic characteristics, and they just weren't presenting themselves. Everything became very jumbled and confused. We were losing sight of what we were doing as a band."

They continued to phone Dave Navarro, the ex-Jane's Addiction guitarist who had already passed on previous offers. Eventually, Chad Smith, Flea and Anthony settled for an unknown guitarist called Jessie Tobias. Jessie was a member of Mother Tongue – a high-gloss ska/metal/funk band – who had only recently been signed to Sony Music. Yet Jesse walked away from the deal in order to play guitar for the Red Hot Chili Peppers. He lasted one month.

"Dave (Navarro) said a funny thing once," Anthony recalls, "when I phoned him up and asked him to join. At the time, he was committed to his new band Deconstruction and I said: 'Well, do you know anyone that you think could be appropriate for all the bases that need to be landed on?'. He answered: 'Yeah, it would be me, I'm the only guy in the world who could do it and I can't do it'. So it was almost like he was taunting me.

"Time went by. This crap happened and I was walking down Sunset Strip with Chad, and I said, 'Chad, what are we going to do? You know we're in a dilemma here, we don't have a guitar player, we need to write music, we need to write songs, we need to express'.

"And he said, 'Well, Dave's gonna join the band'. I said, 'No, Dave's not joining the band'. And he said, 'No, I've got a feeling'. So I said, 'Whaddaya mean you've got a feeling? You're a drummer, you can't have a feeling!'. He said, 'I've just got a feeling Dave's gonna join the band'.

"And about a week later, Dave joined the band."

134

RED HOT CHILI PEPPERS
SUGAR AND SPICE

The Red Hot Chili Peppers had not only found themselves a new guitarist, but they had also recruited a sizeable chunk of cross-counter culture into the deal. On paper it was the perfect marriage, and one that was more than able to take the Chili Peppers into the second half of the decade with their credibility intact.

"At first I was really nervous about it," Dave Navarro told RAW magazine's Artie Nelson, "and then I was really insecure about it, and then I was really excited about it, then I was convinced it was gonna be the greatest thing in the world. "But then when I get too comfortable a feeling it's gonna be so great, I get nervous again. Then I get bored of being nervous... it's a never-ending cycle. It's gonna be what it's gonna be."

The Red Hot Chili Peppers knew that with Dave Navarro aboard, the band's very core would need to be re-defined. There were so many expectations to meet that no-one really knew if it was entirely feasible. They needed to take time out from the rigours of writing, rehearsing and bonding within a city environment.

As the year drew to a close, the Chili Peppers relocated to the infinitely happier climate in Hawaii. It was supposed to be another crash-course in Pepperdom for Navarro – albeit a more luxurious initiation than those afforded John Frusciante, Arik Marshall and Jessie Tobias – and an exercise in faith restoration for Flea, Chad and Anthony. It was only a partial success.

"We thought we'd go to Hawaii," Anthony said, "where we couldn't be disturbed or distracted by telephones and friends and family and we could get on with being a musical masterpiece. But Hawaii was so remote that to some degree we sort of vegetated.

"There's so much vegetation there that we sort of assimilated into the greenery, which was cool. Then we came back here, went up to San Francisco and tried to move into a house where we were going to record... and we got there and we were all ready to get things going and we still had some material to write." In fact the Red Hot Chili Peppers did little in Hawaii except swim, surf, drink and party. The house in San Francisco had been booked by Rick Rubin over Christmas, and the loyal, trusted producer was insisting that work on the record start soon.

'BloodSugarSexMagik' was already two years old. The touring schedule, as well as John Frusciante's departure, Flea's illness and Dave Navarro's arrival, had all delayed the band's sixth album. It was now a new year, and 1994 was already booked with headlining appearances at Woodstock II, the Reading and Sunstroke festivals. There was precious little time to waste on a tropical beach. As the band immersed themselves totally in their creative pool, a new scandal erupted over Anthony Kiedis' sexual antics.

135

136

In January 1994, US spokeswoman for health and human services, Donna Shalala, was said to be "outraged" on learning that Kiedis had been recruited by an AIDS information advert.

The advertisement and radio campaign spearheaded a new initiative by AIDS information bureaus to highlight the threat of the disease. Kiedis volunteered his services for a radio advert, saying: "Remember, you can be naked without being exposed".

Shalala could not believe that the Chili Peppers' frontman could be an entirely appropriate mouthpiece, bearing in mind his four-year-old conviction for sexual battery. The US government ordered the agency to give her a report detailing why it failed to take note of Kiedis' background.

To the Red Hot Chili Peppers, this was just one more example of the moral majority masquerading as caring ambassadors of the nation's morals. Anthony Kiedis' criminal conviction was a matter of public record. Had Donna Shalala taken the trouble to speak directly with the singer, however, she might not have reacted quite so hastily.

By the end of 1994, Anthony Kiedis had willingly taken 5 separate AIDS tests.

"I would never, ever want to give anybody I cared about – even someone I didn't care about – something that would kill them.

"I go to a lot of different doctors. I go to an acupuncturist, and I have a homeopathic doctor. And so a lot of times when I'm going in to find out what chemicals are in my body, I'll just say, 'Do an HIV test while you're at it'. The first one I had was petrifying. I was on pins and needles for days until I found out. The second one was when I started going out with this girl, and her mother was really into finding out that I was OK. And that was a little nerve-wracking. But since then, it hasn't been. Since I stopped using intravenous drugs, I'm in a very low-risk group.

"In this particular case, this ad agency consigned by the government came to me and said, 'Will you do a radio PSA (public service announcement) for the use of condoms?' And I said to myself, 'Well, that sounds like a very productive and positive thing to do'. So they came to our studio, and Flea and Chad and Dave play this sort of swinging jazz groove while I do this spiel about about, 'Here I am wearing my condom when I have sex – every time, not just when it's convenient, not just when my partner thinks of it, but every single time'. Which is something that everybody in the band believes in.

"And the ad agency was very pleased, and the government was very pleased. But then this one woman (Shalala) who was in charge of the whole thing finds out it's me and says 'This guy did something to a girl' – which in reality I did not – and she was very rigid about getting me kicked off the programme.

"From my point of view, everybody loses out. The ironic fact was that I never did what it was that I was accused of."

As writing for the album continued in California, yet another court action was filed against the Red Hot Chili Peppers. This time it was personal.
Jack Sherman had sat on the sidelines watching the band he once played guitar for rise up through the ranks and finally burst through the cloudbase with 'BloodSugarSexMagik'. Their success stuck in his throat. He remembered the circumstances leading up to his dismissal in 1985, and took a long look at his far-from-profitable career.

Finally, Sherman filed against his former bandmates, seeking compensation for unpaid royalties and damages for his dismissal. His lawyers claimed that his contractual agreements had been "fraudulently violated", and that his dismissal had been preceded by a period in which he had been "treated with contempt and subjected to continuous verbal abuse and ridicule and even occasional physical abuse."

This action surprised and upset the Red Hot Chili Peppers. Sherman's legal allegations centred around the sales of their debut, eponymous album, and yet the contracts drawn up at the time could not have been fairer.

Anthony and Flea believed that all song-writing royalties should be split evenly between all four band members regardless of an individual's actual input. The bulk of the music was written by Flea and executed by Jack Sherman and drummer Jack Irons. Anthony was solely responsible for the lyrics. But that contract was more of a brotherly statement. It stipulated that no matter how little anyone actually created, he would still receive the same royalty as his fellow bandmates. Jack Sherman was arguing that this situation was, eight years later, simply not reasonable!

The Red Hot Chili Peppers reacted angrily. Kiedis described him as "a complete asshole!", whilst Lindy Goetz doubted the validity of the claims with more caution.

"Despite numerous requests, he (Sherman) has yet to tell us what he thinks is owed. The case is completely without merit."

Only Jack Irons – the former drummer who played with Sherman on the album – has articulated the band's defence.

"The Red Hot Chili Peppers worked hard, and I only credit Anthony and Flea for that. They've gone through a lot of hardship; it's not like they had overnight success. Jack Sherman made one record with them, and that was it."

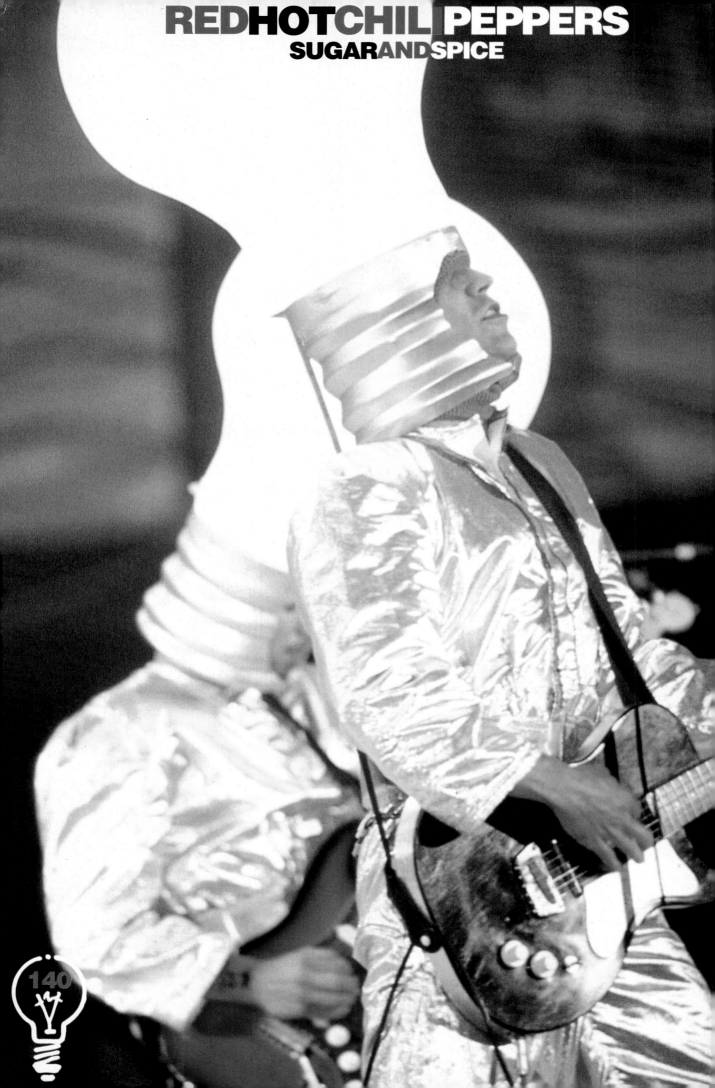

HOT PEPPERS
SUGAR   SPICE

The band brushed aside these incidents and concentrated instead on their music. Despite sketching out nearly 100 ideas with Dave Navarro, time and circumstances were not on the Chili Peppers' side.

"There was a lot of music that needed lyrics," Anthony told NME's Johnny Dee. "There was a lot that needed vocal melodies and rhythms and stuff like that and I was all geared (up)... But when it came to recording, we got our producer and we listened to the sound of the room, so now we've got all of our gear up there, all of our mojo up there, all of our energy was up there ready to go and we said, 'No, This studio will never do'.

"So that was kind of like having the rug pulled out from under you and we came back and went into a studio and recorded all the basics and the shit just sounded slamming. It was really beautiful music that these guys were making and I was doing my scratch vocals and we got ready to go into the overdub portion, and suddenly we realised that Woodstock was three weeks away."

The band effectively iced any further recording schedules in favour of concentrating on their imminent festival shows. It was a heart-stopping opportunity to debut Dave Navarro as well as the future sound of the band itself.

In July, the band made their unofficial debut at two small clubs in Los Angeles. The gigs were unannounced and witnessed by only a handful of regulars. The official launch took place at the enormous Woodstock II festival a week later.

It was a strong but not necessarily awesome display. The weather was against all the bands and the Saugerties farm was a mud-fest. The Chili Peppers tried too hard to make it work, and consequently failed to ignite. Ironically, considering Flea and Anthony's distrust of the European music scene, it was the band's headlining performance at the Reading Festival which cemented their future.

It was also an appearance to quash the endless rumours of a split within the ranks. After such a lengthy period of public inactivity, many journalists had begun to speculate on the situation. Reports that Dave Navarro had quit reached New York, amidst more damaging gossip that Anthony Kiedis had returned to his heroin ways. The old adage of once an addict, always an addict, seemed relevant, and coupled to Navarro's own history of drug abuse in Jane's Addiction, this appeared to be a likely scenario. Numerous management and record company personnel were at pains to point out that nothing could be further from the truth.

The Reading and Sunstroke festivals convinced any remaining pessimists that the Red Hot Chili Peppers had been born again. More importantly, the band knew that they still had the same spark which had ignited them a decade earlier, and had sustained them through tragedy and discomfort, and nurtured their evolution into the kings of crossover. Dressed as light bulbs.

Chapter 15 Epilogue

It's 1995. Everybody is talking about punk rock. Everybody says stuff goes in cycles, yet no-one cares to mention such constants as the Red Hot Chili Peppers. Punk rock is now a million dollar deal and green hair. Punk is now a strictly North American phenomenon and that means it comes with strings attached. Sometimes you can see the strings. Punk is now stuff like Pearl Jam releasing their records on vinyl and not talking to anyone.

Everybody is talking about grunge dying on its feet because they couldn't find a pop star to carry the flag. They only found Kurt Cobain when he died. His face now sells more magazines than when he was touring 'In Utero', because everybody tells you that they knew Kurt would eventually kill himself and nothing sells so much as grave robbing. Elvis knows.

Everybody is talking about a new age of frivolity. People need frivolous baubles to dazzle and strobe, because no-one can afford the luxury of high-brow stimulus and schoolkids are stupid. Tall people are less at risk from heart attacks, and nuclear waste is actually pretty good for you. It's the age of misinformation. People will grow up to disbelieve absolutely everything they are told. Who needs the agents of reason and logic to spoil the virtual reality funfair?

It's 1995. There will always be an excuse for a party. Today Anthony Kiedis is at home, up in the Hollywood hills overlooking Griffith Park. His house is full of mementos and art. His fridge is covered with stickers from around the world. There is a framed photograph of his current girlfriend, taken at her recent High School graduation ceremony. Kiedis is 32 now and the proud owner of an original Dali and several paintings by Robert Williams. The large stone fireplace is sculpted into the shape of a woman's torso, complete with purple glass nipples. He sleeps in his bedroom beneath a huge wooden angel, allegedly erected to protect all who lie below. His huge Harley Davidson motorcycle is parked unobtrusively by the side of the house. Last year Anthony Kiedis bought his father a house in seven acres of land by the side of Lake Michigan. Last year Anthony Kiedis paid for his two sisters to go through college.

"For years," he says, "Flea and I have roamed around the city not having any idea how we were going to go about eating lunch or dinner. When we first hooked up with our manager, we said, 'If you want to manage us, you have to make sure that we eat every day'. That was the big thing. We never had money of our own or houses or cars or anything like that. But in the last few years, everything's changed drastically. Because our ascent was so gradual, we had a lot of time to figure out how we were most comfortable doing what we do. If we'd become tremendously popular after our first record, we'd have disintegrated years ago. But because it happened over the course of five records, we had a lot of time to figure it all out along the way."